WAR! YOU MUST WIN!

BATTLE IS THE SEED FOR TERRITORY

Dr. Jerry A. Grillo, Jr

ISBN: 978-0692348727

The Battle For

Your Future Is Determined By The Warfare You're Willing To Face!

TABLE OF CONTENT

CHAPTER ONE

THE WEAPONS OF WARFARE

God's Battle-Axe

Are you prepared to be God's BATTLE-AXE?

*"Thou art **my battle axe** and weapons of war: for with thee will I break in pieces the nations, and with thee will I destroy kingdoms; And with thee will I break in pieces the horse and his rider; and with thee will I break in pieces the chariot and his rider; With thee also will I break in pieces man and woman; and with thee will I break in pieces old and young; and with thee will I break in pieces the young man and the maid; I will also break in pieces with thee the shepherd and his flock; and with thee will I break in pieces the husbandman and his yoke of oxen; and with thee will I break in pieces captains and rulers." Jeremiah 51:20-23*

T he church has slipped into a state of lethargy in my opinion. In case you don't know what "lethargy" means let me give you the definition; weariness, lazy, fatigued and slow. There is a very popular TV series called, "**The Walking Dead.**" I am always reminded of the church when I watch this show because many who confess to being Christians are in most cases the "**Walking Dead.**" In this show, the dead walk around looking to eat the living.

I was raised in church and have been in ministry for over thirty years. I can honestly say that many just sit in church, seeking to devour the living, not looking to grow or learn the things of God. Religious people are quick to shut down other's change, excitement and joy.

We need to be stirred up! In my opinion, someone needs to move into the auditorium and make some noise. Shout and run and move and cry and shake up the dead. I don't even feel like a success in my preaching if I don't offend someone. Don't misunderstand me. I'm not meaning offense in a bad way, but in the way that will cause change. I want to be God's battle AXE! What about you? I want to shout! I want to let God know and everyone else to know that I AM ALIVE! God is ALIVE!

PLAYERS WIN GAMES

We have become a gathering of people who want to be comforted instead of *confronted*. We've become a people who want to be motivated instead of inspired. We want taming instead of training. People are more focused on being cheered on, instead of being stretched for change. In the church, cheerleading has become more important than coaching.

Coaches decide the results of the games. Cheerleaders decide the motivations of the spectators. Coaches focus on those who are on the playing field while cheerleaders are for those who are sitting in the crowd. Do you see where I'm going? So many are coming to the house of God to sit in the crowd and be cheered into an excited feeling instead of coming to be coached to play the game of life.

When we leave the sanctuary, we enter a battle field where the enemy has been coaching his team on how to influence you, discourage you, defeat you and distract you. Think of the danger you face if all you have gotten on Sunday is a "good 'ole soft sermon" of feel good words. In some cases, people are going to church where a pastor does not even preach out of the word of God. Some have even taken up the resolve to take present day movies and use the themes to teach about current events. We are going to have to have an encounter with something, no, someone larger than the current events if we are going to overcome and survive the end times. That person is God!

Because of this lack of training and discipleship, most people are not mentally, spiritually or physically ready for the enemies that are waiting on us when we leave the gathering, the church service. Many don't know how to fight when they enter the battle field. We are supposed to be God's **battle-axe**! We are God's weapons of war!

It's very dangerous when all we do is try to make people feel good about their lives and wrong decisions; trying to get them to make peace with the trouble in their lives. One of the most deadly things we can do is shorten people's consequences for their wrong decisions. How else are they going to learn if they don't experience the pain of failure?

"It's easier to train and grow children than it is to repair broken adults."

I was helping this person in my church, and it seemed that every time I turned around they needed help. Help with their finances. Help with their addictions. Help in their relationships. I began to become very burdened to why they couldn't get it straightened out. After much thought, the Holy Spirit impressed these thoughts on me. "If you keep shortening their consequences they aren't ever going to change."

God placed on the earth the law of cause and effect for a reason. Then this came to my spirit. *"Son, if you are becoming the source that stops what I'm trying to accomplish in my children, you now become the source that's fighting me, not helping me." I now see you as a problem."*

Sometimes you just have to let people suffer. Allow them to feel the pain of their bad decisions and in doing so you stop them from making the same mistake. All this happens when we live the truth, not just speak it. The opposite is what is happening in the church today. We are trying to calm the raging power of sin by allowing it to be okay, even to the point that the church can't even speak against some really blatant sins without experiencing persecution.

I'll never forget when I was preaching in a particular church for a weekend. I couldn't seem to get the people to respond to anything. The atmosphere seemed to be void of conviction, power and change. The congregation just sat there staring at me. The more I preached the power of change, the more they looked hollow. Some looked like they wanted to kill me. After a couple of services under my belt, I began to question my anointing and the reason for even being sent by God to preach at this particular church. The Holy Spirit impressed on me, *"**I didn't send you here for them, but for him, the Pastor.**"*

I began to ask the pastor questions about his church and his people. I asked him why his people seemed to be so stiff necked to powerful preaching. His answer every time was, "Dr. Grillo, these people are great people, and I just love on them." He said, "I don't preach much on change because I just want to be their poppa!"

Are you kidding me? I looked at him and said, "The Lord says because you refuse to call sin a sin, and speak the truth, **you will love your sheep straight to hell**."

He began to cry and repent, and asked me to help him establish a better government in his church.

TRUTH HURTS BEFORE IT HEALS

Truth never comes easy. The truth is that the truth usually hurts us before it heals or changes us. The real truth can cut! We need to be aware of this, but more importantly, we need to be tough enough to speak the truth no matter what we're feeling for those we're speaking it to.

If we refuse to speak truth because of love, then that love is one sided - your side. *All we're doing is birthing an attitude of contentment and passivity, an attitude of "Well, my life is what it is and that's all it's going to be; let me just try to find anything that will change in it."* But I want to tell you that if you really want **God's love you need to prepare for war!** It's time to go to war… warfare requires battles.

Battle means any fight, struggle or conflict.

If you're in a struggle over anything, **you're in a battle**. You may be having a struggle in your marriage, a struggle over addictions, your finances or over something in your mind. These are battles you have to confront.

- Anything uncontested will flourish.
- Anything you're unwilling to confront grows.
- Anything permitted takes over.

How are you going to survive? How are you going to win if you don't learn how to fight or confront? You need to learn how to get mad, angry and frustrated enough to fight or **hell is going to win**.

Do you want the truth? You may not be able to handle the truth! Here's the truth. Everyone, somewhere is in a conflict, they are in a struggle; somebody, somewhere is fighting an enemy every day in life. They are fighting wrong attitudes. Some are fighting the enemy of wrong lust, some are fighting anger issues and some are fighting to overcome bitterness over things in their past and present hurts. Then there are religious wounds that are running rampant in the church all over this country. People are getting hurt because of religious scars, religious words and rejections. Many come into a place and try to lick each other's wounds and comfort each other's bleeding instead of becoming warriors that show the scars of warfare.

It is time to heal the wounds, heal the bleeding and heal all the tears. Some of you need to trade your tears in for some ashes out of your own pile of pain and start scarring your face and say, *"I am coming up tomorrow with a marked face prepared with a resolve to win! There is no option! Give me liberty, or give me death over this yoke, but I am not carrying this thing any further!"*

You've got to make up your mind that people die in war and if you don't get a resolve to die, you will not fight to live.

- Are you tired of the enemy slapping you around?
- Are you tired of living the same life repeating the same mistakes? Some of you have been fighting the same devil for twenty years!
- Are you exhausted?

Here's the plain truth. You can't begin to go to war over the **new enemies** in your life until you conquer the old ones, the ones from your past. Why should God enlarge your territory? Why would you even consider more territory if you're not winning and controlling what you already possess?

You must realize that there is an enemy you will have to fight at every new level of increase and possession of new territory. Asking God for a larger vision, a larger territory, a greater marriage or greater financial resources means you are waking up the enemies that are assigned to keep you from entering the future you have already been destined for.

Many Christians have forgotten that "Church" should be a training camp for soldiers as much as it is a place for worshippers to gather. They have been lulled into a false mindset that the enemy isn't after them or their purpose. Jesus has conquered Satan in the spiritual realm and in the spiritual arena Satan and His demons are defeated and stripped of spiritual jurisdiction. However, what many fail to realize is that the earth - or natural realm- hasn't been conquered.

Disciples of Christ must recognize and stand in the authority Christ has given us in order to conquer the earth! The spiritual world is waiting on the earthly world to make the connection. This connection is when my faith transcends the natural situation and embraces the spiritual revelation that if I agree with the Word of God, I can control the earth realm again.

Many are trying to enter new territories by having good praise and prayer services. You have to be willing to fight the enemies occupying the territory that you want to possess as your own! If you want a better marriage, you've got to *fight* for a better marriage. If you want a better mind, you've got to *fight* for a better mind. If you want a better attitude, you've got to *fight* for a better attitude. It is not going to be handed to you on a silver platter. It's not going to be handed to you because you came to church and sat among the saints.

REFUGEE CAMP IS CLOSED

We have made the church a camp of refugees too often. If you looked up the word refugee, you would find that it means *a group of people, or a person that is not willing to fight for a religion, land or persuasion.*

Refugees are capable and able to fight for their rights, but they will not. This is a group of people that gather together and refuse to draw weaponry and arms against attrition, tyranny, opposition. Their refusal to fight causes them to be taken into captivity or worse, slaughtered, all because they refuse to defend their lives, lands and families.

Refugee camps are built by others – or a nation - who rise up out of compassion to protect the refugees. That nation sends *their* soldiers and military and drains *their* resources to protect and defend the refugees.

Listen to me. This may be a noble thing to do in the natural...but this is not what the Church was designed for. The Church was **NEVER** meant to be a refugee camp! We are not supposed to build walls of comfort. The church was never created to be the four walls of peace, the four walls of feeling better, or the four walls where you come and leak all of your pain.

The church is the place where God trains His warriors. It is a place to be trained; it is a place for you to fight for religion; it is a place where you learn how to fight for what is right in your marriage, your home and your children. Now I don't know about you, but the devil is not playing fair. He is not playing nice; he's playing nasty. What we need is nice to get up out of the church and a little bit of nasty to get up in some of the Christians! Stop being pretty! Get angry! Get warfare minded! Let's draw some swords! Let's prepare for war!

There's a scripture in the Bible that says that God was angered against His children because He couldn't find any Blacksmiths among them. They had become so comfortable in their peace that they stopped making swords and weaponry and lost the skills. God's anger kindled against them. The more peace you have, the stronger the military has to be.

Thinking about battle is uncomfortable because when you go to war you have to leave family. You have to leave friends, neighbors, mothers and fathers. What are you willing to die for? What are you willing to walk away from to win? What are you willing to put down and say "no" to so that you can say "yes" to your future and "yes" to victory?

Paul's whole life was a battle. In 2 Timothy chapter 4, you can read a scripture where Paul said, *"I am already being poured out as a drink offering and the time of my departure is at hand. I have fought the good fight, I have finished the race, I have kept the faith. Finally there is laid up for me a crown of righteousness which the Lord the righteous judge shall give to me on that day and not to me only, but also to all who have loved His appearing."* Three things Paul said, *"I've fought a fight. I've finished the fight. I've kept my character and my persuasion in the midst of battle."*

Many of us will go to war; we'll start fighting lust, we'll start fighting addiction, but in the middle of the fight we are conquered and lose. Paul said I've fought a good fight. I didn't just fight it; I finished it. I didn't just finish it; I kept my focus in the midst of my problems. I want to get to a place in my life where

I can say to those I'm mentoring, *"Listen, I fought the good fight, I've finished the race and the only thing left for me now is God's applause and my praise."*

Who is to fight in this battle? Everybody is a soldier in the church. In the early days of the revolution, the motto on Britain's flag was "Don't tread on me," and a rattlesnake was its mascot. The message they were sending was, *"We might look small, we might not look like we have much, but you go ahead and step on me and see if I don't bite you with all of the poison within me."* Things may begin to change in your life if you change your countenance, get battle-ready and make the devil nervous by saying, *"Don't mess with me!"*

Jeremiah chapter 51:20 really touches me because it tells me exactly what is going on in my own life. God is talking to Jeremiah about how the enemy has come in and how those who call themselves "God's people" have weakened their positions and minds. They have started to love other gods and build images to worship. Remember, Jeremiah was not a grown man. He was a young man, a teenager. So he's standing there, a teenager, and God told him that He was going to use him and make him His prophet. He told Jeremiah that he would be the mouthpiece of God and a voice to the nations. Jeremiah responded to God by telling Him that he was just a boy and how inadequate he was. God quickly reminded Jeremiah that age makes no difference when His anointing is upon you.

I love the anointing because the anointing isn't qualified by age; it's qualified by willingness. The Holy Ghost in you is the same in everyone. This is why a twelve-year-old can lay hands on someone and have the same authority as a fifty-year-old.

While Jeremiah is thinking about what to do, God tells him, ***"You are My battle-ax and weapon of war,*** *For with you, I will break the nation in pieces. With you, I will destroy kingdoms. With you, I will break in pieces the horse and its rider. With you, I will break in pieces the chariot and its rider. With you, I will break in pieces man and woman. With you, I will break in pieces old and young. With you, I will break in pieces the young man and the maiden. With you, I will also break in pieces the shepherd and his* *flock. With you, I will break in pieces the farmer and his yoke of oxen, and with you, I will break in pieces governors and rulers."*

Paul said it in 2 Corinthians 10:4, *"The weapons of our warfare are not carnal but they are mighty in God..."* It is all about opposition! You are never going to live a life without war. You are never going to live a life with peace unless you're willing to fight everything; whether it's in your marriage, whether it's connected to you, whether it's in your checking account. Some of you right now have battles and hell is trying to bring down your money, your mind and your marriage, but I declare that ENOUGH IS ENOUGH! It's time to become God's battle-ax! You've got to be God's weapon! All the weaponry was paid for at Calvary's tree.

If you look at a sword, the top end looks like a cross. Years ago, most noblemen carried swords and when they would pray they would always pull their sword out, bow their knee, and look at their sword. It represented the cross on the battlefield. On one end was their peace and prayer, but on the other end was what they used to kill and murder what tried to stop what they were doing.

The cross is a weapon, it is a sword. On one end you grab it. That is the end that Jesus was hung on. The end that Jesus hung on is what you cling to, what you hold on to. It is what His death bought for you. His crown was your crown. His scars cleaned you. His stripes healed you; but once you have taken hold of Jesus then you need to turn around and use the Word of God, which is the back-end of that
Cross. It's the blade... the sharp, two-edged sword that cuts and divides truth against lies.

Passivity is over!

You can't fill up a church with passivity. Some of you won't even talk about Jesus, you won't invite anyone to your church and I've heard some say it's because they are afraid that God will move. How can you be afraid that God will move? Are you embarrassed? Well if so, it's obvious that you're not persuaded that He's the God that ought to move.

WORSHIP HAS TURNED INTO LEAKING WOUNDS:

- We are so caught up in our wounds.
- We are so caught up in our struggles.
- We are so caught up in our pains.
- We are crying about our kids.
- We are crying about our money.

We are so focused on our pain and problems that we do not have time at our workplace, homes or even at places of our leisure to talk about the King or speak about God and His greatness. The last verse in Judges says that because they had no king each man loved his own life and did his own thing. If you don't swear allegiance to a king, you will swear allegiance to the god of this world.

You may say that this feels as if I'm attacking you. Well, I am. I'm attacking your reluctance to stand, your passivity to witness, your unwillingness to bring your friend, or walk across the street to your neighbor and tell them that their lives are out of order and invite them to come with you and let you help them get their life equipped for battle.

"In those days there was no king in Israel: every man did that which was right in his own eyes." Judges 21:25

We are in the end times. I believe this more now than ever. They've just voted in congress that all newborn babies can get a chip put in their arm so the government will have the capability to track them. We are in line for the mark of the beast.

We are in line for the Antichrist to take over and a one-world-government to be formed. In America, people need to lose their self-confidence and attitude that we are invincible.

At the time I am writing this book, American money on the European money market has already dropped. It's almost 4-6 to one.

In England, the pound is worth more than the dollar. The economy in this country is in a shaking and it's in a stalemate and if we don't get some Christians who'll draw their swords and pray and get mad, we're going to give up this fight.

It's time to get mad!

The enemy is coming after your kids, he's coming after your money, he's coming after your land, and he's coming after your family, your brother and your sister. We've got to get into the mud of life and FIGHT! FIGHT! FIGHT! It's a battle and you will lose if you lay down.

The battle is not going away

It's a sad day when preachers get up on a rainy Sunday morning and immediately know that the congregation attendance will be down. People use to have to walk to get anywhere. Now, they can't even get up and drive to the House of God. I preached in Mexico years ago in a small village where there were no major stores, not even a stoplight. We were in an open aired building, meaning there were no sides, just roofs. Sitting there with the pastor I looked outside and it was pouring rain. My thought was, *"Well, there won't be a great crowd tonight."* I mentioned to the pastor that very comment. He said *"Oh no, pastor, this place will be full."* To my amazement he was right. That place was packed. I saw people coming from everywhere when I looked out into the dark streets. They walked, some for miles, in the rain and through the mud to get to the place where they knew God was going to meet them. Can you imagine what kind of church services we would have in America if the people had that same committed, sacrificial life?

Truth: We are lazy… We are a self-serving minded people. Have we allowed prosperity to weaken us instead of increasing us? We've made serving God dependent upon our comfort. ***Comfort always creates disorder. Order creates comfort.***

The Bible says, ***"The fear of God is the beginning of wisdom."*** You can't even get wise until you learn to have a healthy fear of God. Fear is honor. We don't really fear God because God has not shown the strong arm of His hand like He did in the Old Testament.

We have become too familiar and too comfortable with God. God's love and mercy has in some ways weakened us. We have taken His graciousness for granted. It's dangerous when we become so impressed with ourselves that we become unimpressed with God! Let's not forget that in reality we are walking dirt; dust that God formed and breathed life into.

Who are we to question God? We are what He made us to be and He made us out of dirt. God gave dirt meaning, purpose and life. Without Him, without His hand we would turn back to soil. Somewhere in all this hype and splendor of prosperity, we've lost the true meaning and respect of our Creator. Why don't we just stop for a moment and put our lives back in perspective... without Jesus we could do nothing; we would be nothing.

*"I am the vine, you are the branches; he who abides in Me and I in him, he bears much fruit, **for apart from Me you can do nothing.**"*
John 15:5

WHAT TO DO WHEN YOU'RE BATTLE HAS BEEN IN A PROLONGED SEASON

The battle may not go away!

People who've fought in war say that those who die were usually the ones that became comfortable on the battlefield. They start forgetting the things they were taught in boot camp. They stop keeping their socks dry and get disease. They forget about the traps that the enemy has set, the land mines that have been buried and the things that have been hidden by the enemy to kill them. They start walking around reckless with a *nonchalant attitude* and become reckless on the battlefield.

I believe we, as Christians, have become reckless in the midst of the battlefield. We just shout and stomp and run and the devil has planted mines all over our lives. You need to get up every day when your feet hit the floor knowing that there is an enemy watching and waiting to take you out! I hope I've made it very clear that **YOU'RE IN A BATTLE!**

There's a problem when the churches focus more on making people feel comfortable than convicted. They spend more time on sermons than on training for battle. I've noticed a serious trend that has developed. Churches that are easy and comfortable, never really preaching about the consequences of life and wrong living are packed, and the ones that do have empty pews. The people have become too soft in this church. We are easily swayed; looking for entertainers instead of anointing. We are more interested in get quick and don't offend churches. No one can tell you the truth, because in reality the truth hurts before it heals. The truth will always reveal the lie that is hiding in the room.

Is this what God sent Jesus to die for? To get people to the nearest spiritual buffet line and stuff them with something to eat and send them home to lie on the couch and wait to be slaughtered. *There's a problem!*

At the *Favor Center Church,* where I pastor, I'm not going to shorten our praise and worship, nor am I going to water-down what's going on in the spirit realm. I'm not going to take someone to a back room when it's time to cast out devils, or am I going to hide them in some small room for a private deliverance session.

The enemy doesn't do his work in private. He flashes his work, his perversion in public. If he came in your life in public, let's cast him out in public. That's what Jesus did. He made a public spectacle of him. I want to get up in the enemy's face and tell him we are not afraid! I want to do whatever it takes to win this battle. I am not going to fight nice.

When it comes to the devil, I am going to quote General George Patton, *"God better have mercy on my enemy, 'cause I won't."*

It's time for us to get angry. It is time to get ready to oppose all the enemies' attacks. We need to charge his strongholds. We need to break down his chains and his dark walls. Once he is in retreat, we need to chase him down and kill everything attached to him. We need to take everything he stole back! Maybe you're thinking, *"Well, that's radical. That doesn't sound very kind..."* Here's my thought! Why should we be nice?

- Do you think cancer is kind? That's from him.
- Do you think poverty's kind? The enemy is the reason for poverty. Can you think of anything that is good about poverty?
- Is there anything good about anger, confusion, rejection, bitterness or emotional wounds? These are the results of sin and the fall of man.
- Is there anything lovely about parents leaving their children and forcing the grandparents to raise them?

One time I saw this woman with many children. I asked her why she had so many kids and where their father was. She told me, *"I don't even know who their daddy is."* I said, *"Do you mean to tell me that you've got this child by one man and this one by another and this one by another?"* Her answered stunned me. She said, **"Uh-huh, I sure do. You see this one's a check and that one's a check and that one's another check."**

Here's the irony of it all; men are so stupid because they keep sleeping with these kinds of women and helping them write the check. She had those children not so she could raise them and train them and nurture them, but so she could live a life of convenience and money at the expense of those children. How sad. How crazy and sick is this way of living? Who is behind it all? The enemy, the devil, who is the one we try to ignore. He is the one we try to keep in private. He's the one driving all this confusion and sin. What does the church do? **Nothing!**

GOD'S SYSTEM IS WARFARE NOT WELFARE

When Joshua's reign was coming to the end, God didn't remove all the enemies. He wanted to keep some around so that the children that were coming up would grow into soldiers and learn how to fight for what was theirs. God is not always removing the enemy.

"I also will no longer drive out before them any of the nations which Joshua left when he died, so that through them I may test Israel, whether they will keep the ways of the Lord, to walk in them as their fathers kept them, or not." Therefore the Lord left those nations, without driving them out immediately; nor did He deliver them into the hand of Joshua." Judges 2:21-23

"Now these are the nations which the Lord left, that He might test Israel by them, that is, all who had not known any of the wars in Canaan. (This was only so that the generations of the children of Israel <u>might be taught to know war</u>, at least those who had not formerly known it)." Judges 3:1-2

I have never noticed this before. God left a residue of the enemy to keep them on battle alert. Just for discussion sake, could it be that God isn't going to kill or remove all of the problems in our lives, problems such as addiction, lust, sin and pleasures?

Maybe He's not going to let the crisis in your life completely leave so that you will never live a life without conflict. Maybe God was trying to teach His people to always be ready for battle.

He left those things there as a test.

Teenager, you're never going to get up and go to school without someone trying to offer you drugs or a life of disobedience. The temptation of premarital sex will always be there. Mom and Dad, temptations and desires for divorce, sin and anger aren't ever going to leave your life. They are there to test us and make sure we are always on guard.

Maybe you have made decisions in your past that birthed unhealthy desires. Those desires may never fully go away. You better learn how to go to war with it every day and don't get mad. It wasn't God who made you do it in the first place. He didn't invite it in, you did. Your body wasn't made to be addicted to anything and if it is, it's because you forced your body to like it.

Now you will have to go to battle and force these things out of your life.

KNOW YOUR ENEMY

Decide to go to war early in life! You've got to know your enemy. This is a fact; your enemy is not a human. You're not fighting a wife or a husband. You're not fighting drugs or addictions. You're not fighting lust and desires. You have an enemy, but that enemy isn't anything you can see or touch. Those are pawns your enemy has chosen to use to break your focus. He wants you to get so mad at the wrong thing so that you never go after the real enemy. Your real enemy is an ex-employee of Heaven. His name is Lucifer. He is known by many names such as serpent and deceiver. The Bible says he does not come looking like the devil or the way the world tries to depict him. He comes robed in flesh and appears to be, as the Bible describes, "An angel of light." You'll be caught off guard and captured by the enemies' devices if you're not battle-ready. He'll look like the church, talk like the church, and act like a Christian. He'll be religious and know the word of God enough to deceive you because you don't know it enough to bring his lies to the surface and expose the truth. He'll have you so embedded in religion that when you go to rebuke him, in actuality you'll be speaking to your own self. Why? It will be you that you have to rebuke. Deception is one of hell's greatest weapons! Another one of his great weapons is fear.

- Fear to fight.
- Fear to stand.
- Fear to try.
- Fear will stop you every time from succeeding in your future.

5 PURPOSES OF WARFARE:
1. ***To paralyze God's plans for your life.*** Expect the enemy to oppose the Godly plans you have in your future. The enemy will find what you are attracted to the most. He will

use whatever he thinks you're fascinated with. He'll use friends to pressure you if you want to be adored. He'll use whatever is at his disposal to paralyze your plans. You must protect your plans. Be very cautious on who you share your dreams and goals with. Your enemy is in the crowd listening.

2. ***He wants you to abort all of your dreams.*** The day you stop dreaming is the day you stop living. I don't care how old you are; get a dream for your life because when you decide the destination, your mind will create the map to get there. Hell knows the beauty and power of how you were created and he wants to abort every dream you have. The word "abortion" implies that conception has already occurred. God has already sown His dream into you and the only way to get it out is for you to abort it. A woman who has an abortion consents to allowing foreign objects to enter where life is trying to grow, then murder the potential and future of a seed. Be careful who and what you allow in your life. It might be a weapon of the enemy sent to abort the seed of destiny God has placed inside of you.

3. ***The enemy wants to squash your hope.*** You become depressed when hope is gone. Depression is a clue you believe tomorrow will not be any better than today. Suicidal thoughts enter a mind without hope. You kill your dreams if you kill yourself. A graveyard is full of unfulfilled dreams, hopes and potential. You lose your faith when you lose your hope and your purpose. You'll settle for a life of mediocrity when faith is gone.

4. ***He wants to shatter your influence, your character and place it into question.*** He wants you to become so messed up by your words that when you do try to get it right and turn things around, your character is always in question. We are reliable by our character; we are known by what we say. If we never do what we say, eventually what we say can't be believed. We say so much in the Kingdom of God and do so little. You have to prove yourself after you've sown the seeds of dishonesty and doubt.

However secret, the enemy is in the beginning in letting you get away with things by telling you they mean nothing. He will expose you in the end. Satan wants everyone to know what you've done. God has no focus on exposing us. His word says He wants to cover us. Protect us. Hide us in His secret place. That's the power of redemption. God says in His word that He would take our sins and throw them into the sea of forgetfulness.

"Who is a God like You, who pardons iniquity And passes over the rebellious act of the remnant of His possession? He does not retain His anger forever, Because He delights in unchanging love. He will again have compassion on us; He will tread our sins underfoot and hurl all our iniquities into the depths of the sea. You will give truth to Jacob And unchanging love to Abraham, Which You swore to our forefathers From the days of old." Micah 7:18-20 NASB

"For I will forgive their wickedness and will remember their sins no more." Hebrews 8:12 NIV

OH, God prepare our hearts and minds for battle!
It's time for war!

CHAPTER TWO

WARFARE
OVER
YOUR HEART

W hen it comes to life, there are some things you better learn swiftly. *Life is not fair. Life is full of struggle. Life is a battlefield.* If you desire a great life then **PREPARE FOR WAR!**

Nothing in life seems to happen just for the sake of happening. I believe everything that's happening in your life is going to

- Train you.
- Grow you.
- Prepare you for your destiny.

God is not blinded by our bad decisions. He is all knowing. He is all-powerful. He is the epitome of wisdom. With that in mind, do you think that our bad decisions have stumped His great plan for our lives? I don't think so. I believe that God went to the end of your life and saw all of your mistakes and flaws, then went back to the place where you were the seed growing in the soil of your mother's womb. When you came out of your mom, God stood over your life and said I've seen it all. I've seen your flaws, your failures and your craziness, and I want you to know, "I STILL CALL YOU BLESSED!"

I've learned this in life. Everyday isn't going to be a great day, but God will be great in everyday!

God has placed destiny in us. He has purposed for us to walk in a life of abundance, but that doesn't erase the fact that we are at WAR. Life is as much a battlefield as it is love, joy and fun. We are waking up every day in a spiritual hostile environment. It's not only the spirit world trying to defeat us; the natural world has its enemies as well. We have to fight the warfare over health, warfare over families, warfare over words, warfare over deadly feelings and warfare over our thoughts. We are in some kind of battle every day. The person who doesn't get up and believe this every day, is the person who begins to let down their guard. The enemy infiltrates the camp when that happens. He doesn't announce his attack; he slowly worms his way into all areas of your life that have been unguarded until he has possessed those areas. Then He'll begin to defeat you.

"Above all else, **guard your heart,** *for everything you do flows from it." Proverbs 4:23 NIV*

The World English Bible says it is *"the wellspring of life."*

Your heart is one of the most important organs in your natural body as well as the spiritual. The Bible speaks often of the heart and your mind. There's a part of your mind that, when activated, can be felt in your heart. For instance, when I sense the spirit of the Lord enter into a worship service or my prayer time or even when I'm driving by myself and begin to worship, I don't feel Him in my mind; I feel God in my Heart. Thus we need not to take away the power of the heart and feelings in understanding how God works. It is not your experience, knowledge or skills that matter most when it comes to the spirit; it is your Heart!

I can testify that when my heart is hurting, wounded, lonely, and aching, nothing seems to matter but to calm it, comfort it, and heal it. That is the reason we need to guard our heart above all else. Protecting the feelings of our heart is very important if we want to walk in a happy and fulfilled life. The word I'm looking for is joy. When we experience God lead joy, nothing that happens can last in our heart because the joy of the Lord will always find its way in to encourage us.

4 REASONS YOU SHOULD GUARD YOUR HEART:

1. **Because our heart is extremely vulnerable**. When something is vulnerable it needs to be guarded.
2. **The heart is extremely valuable**. We don't guard worthless things. I put my garbage out the night before it is

scheduled to be picked up every week I don't sit up watching it in case someone wants to steal it. Why? Because it is trash…it is worthless to me!

3. **Your Heart is the source to all feelings**. King Solomon said it is the "wellspring of life." In other words it is the source of what you are feeling. Your feelings flow into thoughts, words, and actions.

   Think of your heart as a watered spring that feeds all other waters in your life. If I dam up the spring, I stop the flow of emotions. If I poison that spring, the flow becomes toxic. Now the feelings become deadly. Everything depends on the condition of that spring. If your heart is unhealthy, it has an impact on everything else. It threatens your family, your friendships, your ministry, your career and indeed your legacy. It is very important to guard.

4. **Your Heart is under constant attack.** The phrase, "guard your heart," implies that you are living in a combat zone! If you are not careful, you will experience casualties.

Many of us are blinded and oblivious to the reality of this conflict and warfare. WE have an enemy who is bent on our destruction physically, emotionally and spiritually. He not only opposes God, but he opposes everything that is aligned to, and with, God's truths and divine purposes.

Satan uses all kinds of weapons to attack our heart. They come in many different settings, relationships and decisions. He can use disappointments, discouragements, and unfulfilled expectation to pollute your heart. He will flood your heart with the thoughts of failure and criticism.

You might have your own story about how Satan has tried to defeat you. This is why if you and I are going to win…*if we are going to survive…we must guard our hearts.*

CHAPTER THREE

WARFARE OVER YOUR LIFE

Life Is A Battlefield!

*arfare is inevitable.*

- Warfare will always be a part of your life.
- Warfare will always surround a life that is blessed.
- Warfare will always surround a life that walks in faith.

You must understand that all advancement will create warfare in your life. You must prepare to fight. Don't lie down and cry about it. Don't give up. Stand up and fight! Anything in your life worth having is always worth fighting for. Enemies are real. The enemy we face today is real.

Wars are not won when someone dies for what they believe in; they are WON when those we fight die for what they believe in.

I was raised in church. People in church today are not like the people I was raised around. Today, there tends to be this underlying attitude that we should die for our cause. This is true to some degree. Many have died for their convictions. Many have died for our freedom. I am not cheapening nor dishonoring those who have died for our freedoms and rights. Of course, if it came down to it I hope and pray I would lay down my life for Christ. However, if I understand the Bible clearly, Jesus laid down his life so I wouldn't have to. Jesus commanded me to live!

*"The thief does not come except to steal, and to kill, and to destroy. **I have come that they may have life**, and that they may have it more abundantly." John 10:10 NKJV*

"The thief comes only in order to steal and kill and destroy. I came that they may have and enjoy life, and have it in abundance (to the full, till it overflows)." John 10:10 AMP

Do you see the command? It is to live a victorious and full life; a life that is full of abundance, overflow, and increase. I don't know about you, but I am planning on living that kind of life.

I was sitting in a restaurant one day and had to excuse myself to visit the restroom. While I was in there, I saw a tract lying on the floor. I picked it up and read the title. Here's what it said in big bold print. ARE YOU READY TO DIE?

My first thought was, "No, I'm not ready to die."

We have spent the last fifty years adapting to a gospel of death. Many people make death their focus when talking about salvation. We have to scare them by talking about death. Yes, we should prepare people for eternity, but what about their life on earth?

What if I live fifty more years? The question we need to be asking is-ARE YOU READY TO LIVE? Let's start preaching a gospel of life. The gospel that Jesus died for was the gospel of prosperity, the gospel of healing and deliverance. Jesus gave up His life so we wouldn't have to give up ours. Jesus said it out of his own mouth. *"My yoke is easy and my burdens are light..."* It's time to fight for life! It's time to live and not die.

Wars aren't won through death. Yes, death is a part of warfare. Someone had to die, but no soldier enters battle with the mindset to die. Fight, yes! Die, no!

We need to stop preaching a gospel that promotes death and start preaching the gospel that promotes victory in times of war. Yes, we are going to have to face the battlefield every day of our lives. Warfare will always be a part of life, but I don't have to get up and expect to die in this war; I want to live. I'm going to live and not die. I plan on seeing tomorrow every single day.

"No man can sit down and withhold his hands from the warfare against wrong and get peace from his acquiescence." Woodrow T. Wilson

"There is only one tactical principle which is not subject to change. It is to use the means at hand to inflict the maximum amount of wounds, death and destruction on the enemy in the minimum amount of time." General George Patton

I really like this quote. Get in the battle and get out as quickly as possible. The longer you stay in a battle the more fatigued you become. The enemy we are fighting thrives on our fatigue. He uses it to weaken our faith, our resolve and our conviction of why we are fighting in the first place. Battle fatigue causes you to stop fighting the real enemy and to start fighting those who are close to you.

I have witnessed this in my own life. My tiredness causes me to start fighting and resenting my children, my wife and even my calling and ministry. Get in and do as much damage as you can and then get out. Take time to recoup, to regroup and to relax.

THE BATTLEFIELDS

All warfare has to be fought through battles. Every battle has to be in a certain place and on a certain valley or hill. Some say those who always have the high ground are those who usually have the advantage in a battle. Though being on the high ground does give you an advantage, it doesn't always guarantee you will win the battle.

Battle is defined by the combat between opposing forces representing major components of total forces committed to the military campaign, used to achieve specific military objectives.

A battle always has as its purpose the reaching of a mission goal by use of military force.

A victory in the battle is achieved when one of the opposing sides forces the other to abandon its mission, is forced to surrender its forces, have its forces rerouted, forced to retreat or rendered militarily ineffective for further combat operations.

When two parties meet to fight this battle out, this is called the battlefield.

Another way to define a battle is when two parties want the same thing. They will either have to negotiate for them or go to war over them.

Facts about battle:
1. Never allow the enemy to decide when you should fight.

2. Never allow the enemy to decide where to fight.
3. Never go to war where there are no spoils.
4. Never engage on the battlefield without a plan, a strategy.
5. Avoid ambushes at all cost. When found in an ambush, charge the enemy swiftly and without hesitation.
6. Only fight with weapons you have approved in advance.
7. Never try to fight someone else's battles.

"This charge and admonition I commit in trust to you, Timothy, my son, in accordance with prophetic intimations which I formerly received concerning you, so that inspired and aided by them you **may wage the good warfare,** *Holding fast to faith (that leaning of the entire human personality on God in absolute trust and confidence) and having a good (clear) conscience. By rejecting and thrusting from them [their conscience], some individuals have made shipwreck of their faith."* 1 Timothy 1:18-19 AMP

Paul tells Timothy to fight a good warfare, keep his faith and avoid those who have shipwrecked the faith of others through their lives and voices. We have to avoid certain people to fight this war properly. We must especially watch out for those who are unwilling to pay the price to be a good soldier. They will be the ones who will desert you on the battlefield.

"[Consider this:] What soldier at any time serves at his own expense? Who plants a vineyard and does not eat any of the fruit of it? Who tends a flock and does not partake of the milk of the flock?" 1 Corinthians 9:7 AMP

TEAR DOWN ALL STRONGHOLDS:

"For the weapons of our warfare are not physical [weapons of flesh and blood], but they are mighty before God for the overthrow and destruction of strongholds, [Inasmuch as we] refute arguments and theories and reasonings and every proud and lofty thing that sets itself up against the [true] knowledge of God; and we lead every thought and purpose away captive into the obedience of

Christ (the Messiah, the Anointed One), Being in readiness to punish every [insubordinate for his] disobedience, when your own submission and obedience [as a church] are fully secured and complete." 2 Corinthians 10:4-6 AMP

The word 'battle' appears 170 times in the King James Version. The word 'war' appears 225 times. The words 'warfare' and 'soldier' appear 5 times. If you read the Bible, especially the Old Testament, there are all kinds of stories of battles that took place. It is obvious that God is about us engaging in a conflict to win.

Most of you, like me, can say that you have experienced a lot of warfare. I can testify that most of my ministry and most of my life has had warfare. I cannot imagine one time in my life where I didn't have some kind of a battle I had to win in order to succeed. I have experienced warfare over my finances, my home life, my marriage, my church, writing books, television ministry and more. Nothing just seems to come easy for me. Growing up with dyslexia made learning a challenge. I read at the 8th grade level when I graduated High School. Reading has always been a task for me. I jokingly say, *"I can write books; I just can't read them."*

"What doesn't kill you will only make you stronger." In reality, this is not a cliché; this is truth.

God allows warfare to take place when He wants to refine your skills. Struggle produces strength. Pressure reveals what is on the inside of you. Anything you're becoming is the result of pressure. The only way to monitor how you're going to act and react in life is to monitor how you handle warfare, crisis and struggle. I believe that sometimes God lets the mess continue and maybe even increase just to prepare us for bigger tomorrows. I want you to win in every situation. There's nothing that happens to you that God isn't keeping the door cracked to free you from. Don't panic in times of pressure! Don't run, don't complain, just stand and give God his rightful place. Open your mouth and praise him. **"Turn you panic into praise!"**

Get this in your spirit... **Christ has already won the spiritual war**. We have to win in the realm of the physical world. Remember, sometimes all we have to do is survive the battles of life. In the end we win, if we survive the battles. Remember, battles come almost every day. Not every battle is spiritual. Sometimes they're just life's battles, struggles and problems. Use your faith in all areas.

BATTLE IS PROOF YOU'RE CONVINCED YOU CAN WIN!

Warfare develops things in people that would never be developed had they not been through a battle. Battle creates a resolve and brotherhood that transcends even blood. I have witnessed men and women who have fought together in war and when they see each other, they have a different kind of bond than just living around each other or growing up together. They have a bond that is stronger than family. They fought together and were willing to die to protect the other. No greater love is found than a person who is willing to die for another (John 15:13). Battle and warfare produce the strongest bonds.

Battle is the seed for territory

There is no advancement without battle. I'm a firm believer that most things never change on their own. If you desire change it will require your willingness to do something about it. Change is not automatic! Therefore, my conclusion about change is there is no change without a battle. If you want to see change in any area of your life, you're going to have to walk through, live through and survive a season of struggle. We can't even walk in faith without being willing to fight a battle. We must make up our minds that we are willing to fight for territory and increase. You can't actually walk in freedom unless you fight for it. You will not experience the power of freedom unless you have fought for it. You must be the one who takes up an offense against the mediocrity of your life...the fight! The conflict is the place where we decide the battle will begin. We will build our faith in that place. There is a difference between fighting to defend something and fighting to win. It's the same as playing around or playing to win! I want my enemies to know that I am not playing around; I am playing to WIN. How about you?

Battle is the proof you are ready for change. Battle is a clue you are ready for tomorrow's increase. Battle is our seed for control and territory. Those who won't fight are cowards. God has no room in the Kingdom for cowards. In the book of Revelation 21:8, Jesus places the cowardly into the same line up with....well read it below and see what I'm talking about.

"But the cowardly, unbelieving, abominable, murderers, sexually immoral, sorcerers, idolaters, and all liars shall have their part in the lake which burns with fire and brimstone, which is the second death." Revelation 21:8 NKJV

Look at it in The Living Translation.

*"**But cowards who turn back from following me**, and those who are unfaithful to me, and the corrupt, and murderers, and the immoral, and those conversing with demons, and idol worshipers and all liars-their doom is in the Lake that burns with fire and sulphur. This is the Second Death." Revelation 21:8 TLB*

God has no room for those who won't enter the battlefield and fight for Him or for their change. In the Greek, the word 'cowardly' is translated from timid or fearful. Timid and fearful people lack confidence and faith. Don't misunderstand me; fear is always present when faith is around. The proof that faith is required is the fear you feel in any given decision or situation. Never assume that fear will leave your mind or your life.

You have to conquer your fears for faith to work. Courage is the result of performing in the face of fear. I've read many stories about wars and battles. The one thing that catches my attention is that great soldiers do not seek to be great. They are the ones who performed under fire and fear. They did what was necessary even when the odds were stacked against them. They charged a gun or carried the wounded. They did what was necessary and in the end proved to be courageous.

We are the same. We must understand that fear, confusion and trouble will never leave us; but we must show courage. We must still perform under attack. We must stand and do what is necessary and we will become great soldiers in the end. The proof that you are a good soldier is the battles you have fought in and lived through.

The church has changed. The people of God have changed. They seem to have lost their fight. The need to show off is stronger than the need to engage in the fight and do what is necessary to win.

"We've always needed God from the very beginning of this nation, but today we need Him especially. We're facing a new kind of enemy. We're involved in a new kind of warfare and we need the help of the Spirit of God. The Bible's words are our hope..." Billy Graham

This is so true. We are engaged in a different kind of warfare. A new kind of enemy exists. We're not just fighting hell; we have now turned on each other.

QUALIFICATIONS OF A CENTURION

I read a book that really convicted me. The title was "The Centurion Principles," written by Colonel Jeff O'Leary. Let me quote this book from pages 1-6.

"First we must understand that very few of us are willing and able to become Centurions. However we need to strive to be one for the Kingdom of God.

The Legionnaire was promoted to the rank of Centurion *based on at least sixteen years of combat service and valor at the point of the spear.*

* He had to be able to carry ninety pounds of equipment at

least twenty miles per day.

* He had to be able to train in the harshest conditions.

* He was required to equip himself at his own expense and pay for his own food, clothing, bedding, boots, arms, armor and his dues to the burial club.

* He was skilled in engineering and building in addition to being the finest combat soldier.

* He had to enlist for twenty-five years, after which a cash payment and small plot of land were provided (unless the treasure was short of cash, in which case, commitment to service was involuntarily extended).

* Death was the penalty for fleeing during battle or faking illness to avoid battle.

* Minor offenses were the loss of body parts.

* The Centurion always led his troops from the front, never from the rear.

We are in desperate need for battle ready leaders in this 21st century America. We thirst for such leaders to rise to the occasion. We need leaders who are guided by what is right and not what is popular, what is honorable rather than what is legal and what is self-sacrificial rather than what is self-serving.

We need battle skilled and battle proven leaders who we are proud to call our own. We live in an age where "image is everything." In leadership, this model has produced empty shells from presidents to parents, senators to schoolteachers and politicians to pastors.

CONFRONT OR REMAIN CONFUSED

Confusion is the number one weapon the enemy will use on us. He will do what he can to confuse and deceive us. His deception is based on your fear to try and your fear to change. The enemy studies your weaknesses and exploits them. He is aware that strength against strength usually produces no winners. Thus, he moves toward where we have revealed what we are weak or fearful in. That is why we must learn how to fail and get up and try again. Never ignore the battle.

"Victory teaches the simple, failure teaches the wise; success teaches a few lessons, failure teaches a thousand lessons; study the lessons of the defeated."

God has added to the equation the room to fail. ***Without failure there would be no need for a savior.*** God knows that the failure we survive can produce what we need to succeed even greater in our future. Failure becomes an education on how to defeat our enemy when we face him again. Here's the truth... **you will face him again, I promise.**

"...No matter the facts, man will believe the truth that most pleases him. Make your enemy believe the truth that most pleases him and then you can do anything to him." Thomas Beacon

I heard someone say don't be afraid to let your enemy underestimate you. But be ready to act when he moves on his miscalculation.

HABITS CAN REVEAL WEAKNESS

"Study your enemy until you are absolutely certain of his habits. In his habits you will find his weakness."

What you are doing daily is deciding what you are becoming permanently.

*"One who knows the enemy and **knows himself** will not be in danger in a hundred battles." Sun Tzu*

You must be willing to face reality. You must be willing to look past fantasy and look at the real you, the real issues, the real crisis and the real problem. In doing so you will discover what your weaknesses are. This is not a bad thing. It is not a bad thing to discover where you are weak and where you struggle. This little bit of information will help you in protecting those areas you would not have protected without knowing what the 'real' was.

Self-Interrogation

Those who will self-interrogate will be the winners in most conflicts. They have already been through their own fire...their own scrutiny...their own criticism. The willingness to take a hard and good look at your present situation and weakness will give you an extremely high edge in warfare.

Study yourself, study your enemy and this will build the necessary ingredients to produce victory on the battlefield.

Study is the seed for knowledge:

When General Patton defeated Rommel's tanks in a battle, he cried out. *"I read your book...!"*

Patton was willing to do what other leaders weren't. *"Winners are always willing to do regularly what average people do occasionally."* In the end, the willingness of Patton to study his enemy gave him the advantage that he needed to turn the tides to his favor.

Up until this battle, Rommel had never lost a battle. Rommel had never lost a conflict or battle until facing Patton. But after someone read Rommel's book and studied his ways, he was defeated.

General Patton studied his enemy before he entered the battlefield. Patton knew his enemy and defeated him because of this information. Study was the seed for victory. Winners never lose because they understand that sometimes you win and sometimes you learn. Yes, I changed the word lose to the word learn. If you adapt to this way of thinking, then every loss is nothing more than an education for something better.

CHAPTER FOUR

WARFARE
OVER YOUR
ENEMY

T o engage in a battle, you have to have an opponent who is set on opposing your freedom, your belief system, your dreams and your advancement.

A battle occurs when two parties want the same thing. Life will never be void of enemies. I wish it were not so. Truly, enemies can cause a lot of pain and heartache. Enemies come in ways you would never expect in the church world. They do so in the name of their gospel. There is no enemy greater to the advancement of life as a Christian rising up to attack another. I've had my share of those kinds of enemies. They are not worth going to war with. There are no spoils when you battle against other people. I believe the real warfare is against an unseen force that uses humans as its guinea pig.

*"...be strong in the Lord [be empowered through your union with Him]; draw your strength from Him [that strength which His boundless might provides]. Put on God's whole armor [the armor of a heavy-armed soldier which God supplies], that you may be able successfully to stand up against [all] the strategies and the deceits of the devil. **For we are not wrestling with flesh and blood** [contending only with physical opponents], but against the despotisms, against the powers, against [the master spirits who are] the world rulers of this present darkness, against the spirit forces of wickedness in the heavenly (supernatural) sphere. Therefore put on God's complete armor, that you may be able to resist and stand your ground on the evil day [of danger], and, having done all [the crisis demands], to stand [firmly in your place]. Stand therefore [hold your ground], having tightened the belt of truth around your loins and having put on the breastplate of integrity and of moral rectitude and right standing with God, And having shod your feet in preparation [to face the enemy with the firm-footed stability, the promptness, and the readiness produced by the good news] of the Gospel of peace. Lift up over all the [covering] shield of saving faith, upon which you can quench all*

the flaming missiles of the wicked [one]. And take the helmet of salvation and the sword that the Spirit wields, which is the Word of God." Ephesians 6:10-17 AMP

We have an enemy. He is vicious and will take no prisoners. His job is to steal, kill and destroy (John 10). The enemy we fight has been fighting humans for thousands of years. He has mastered how to deceive us. His weapon is lies laced with truth.

There will be some form of resistance no matter what we do in life. Truth is always opposed by lies. Faith is resisted by fear. The adversary of increase is poverty. The counterpart of goodness is evil. There is always a counterpart to anything and they will always war against one another. This is not necessarily a bad thing for without one, the other wouldn't have any meaning in life. There can't be one without the other. They push against each other to produce the wave of change and decision.

* The Common is always resented by the Uncommon.
* The Impure always despise the Pure of Heart.
* The Unholy hate the Holy.
* The Lazy resent the Diligent.

Two sides will always exist in our world. The light has no meaning without the darkness. God is light (John 1) and uses the darkness to hide himself in it. Darkness is where God does his greatest work of restoration. It is in the dark room of the Holy of Holies where the blood was sprinkled. This was where God performed His greatest act of love and postponed the children of Israel's sins for a year.

DARKNESS IS NOT ALWAYS EVIL

It is in darkness where many of us have been found and changed. Think for a moment of how you, or someone you know, were changed in the darkest hour of their life. What should have caused death and destruction really pushed you to seek the light. There is no desire or need for light unless we first begin to dislike the dark places in our lives. I know for a fact that in those places, I become comfortable with the illumination of revelation.

It makes sense to think that God allows these moments in our lives to drive us to seek something more and something better. It is in these hard places where the warrior awakens and desires to fight the battle to gain what is ahead. When we become frustrated with the whips of the enemy, the passion within us rises up to seek the land of promise. The despising of one place causes us to look for a better place. We begin to discern the enemies in our lives that are holding us in the dark places because we have been destined for the light.

DEVELOPED IN THE DARKNESS

Film is not developed in the light. Pictures are captured by a camera through the light, but the film is not processed in the light. The light captures many of us; we are drawn to it like a moth. But after we have encountered the light, God places us in the dark room of development. We are being processed to full color in this time of hiding. Just as the film has to go through a process, we do also. Consider this thought and picture in your mind the process of being in a dark room. There are trays of chemicals and solutions that each film must be placed in for a certain amount of time. It would seem that these liquids would cause damage to the film...but it is absolutely necessary for development.

Our lives are like the film. The more we stay in the dark room - void of light - the more clarity will be developed.

I am sure those times will be hard. You are going to sense a desire to quit, giving in and giving up. Look around your dark room right now. Red light is the only light that does not over expose or rob us of our clarity. Red, the color of blood; Christ's blood was red. We are to focus on the blood of Christ when we are placed in the dark room of development.

God uses crazy things in our lives to drive us to our God given destiny. He uses darkness, storms, crises and enemies.

FACTS ABOUT AN ENEMY:

1. ***God expects us to stir up enemies everywhere we go.*** *"And you will be hated by all men for My name's sake." (Matthew 10:22)*

2. ***God instructs us to anticipate enemies while we are on our journey to destiny.*** (Matthew 10:16)

3. ***God warns us ahead of time that people will become our enemies.*** *"But beware of men; for they will deliver you up to the councils, and they will scourge you in their synagogues; and ye shall be brought before governors and kings for my sake, for a testimony against them and the Gentiles.*
   (Matthew 10:17,18)

4. ***The enemy fears God.*** *"Let God arise, let His enemies be scattered..." (Psalms 68:1)*

5. ***Your enemy is anyone who attempts to interfere with your God given assignment.*** Watch out for those who want to slow you down. Those who try hard to change your focus.

6. ***Your enemy is anyone who resents your willingness and desire for increase.*** People who have a problem with prosperity have a hint of deception in them. They have been deceived by the deceiver and thus have a hint of the deceiver in them. When David entered the battlefield and was willing to fight Goliath it was his older brother who stood up to oppose him. However Eliab had been hearing Goliath taunt the armies of God for days. He wouldn't stand and fight but got mad at someone else when they were willing to.

7. ***Your enemy can be anyone who becomes jealous over your progress.***

8. ***Your enemy is anyone or anything that weakens your focus for change.*** When God starts dealing with your willingness to change, watch out for those who become resistant to it. If your change involves your conviction and your sacrifice then why are they the ones who are offended and mad? Because your change shows them they are lacking theirs.

9. *Your enemy is anyone who strengthens a personal weakness God is trying to remove.* I have witnessed people who are trying to overcome something that have a harder time dealing with their friends than with the issue itself. Their friends become angry when they decide to stop living wrong and start living right. They start trying to convince you why you should not change, why you should not remove those things you are trying to remove, why you are abnormal for becoming so focused on church or on God. They are now your enemy.

10. *Your enemy is anyone who attempts to weaken your faith.* All you have to do is hear someone question your decision to start doubting your convictions. Be cautious of those around you who always challenge your decisions and convictions. Haven't you noticed that as soon as you decide to go on a diet someone wants to bake you your favorite cake?

11. *Your enemy is anyone who loves to always bring up your past and make it the center of conversation.* Stop discussing your past with people, especially if you've placed your past under the blood of Jesus and received forgiveness. My persuasion is to only bring up your past to help others conquer the same areas you've conquered. Use it as your weapon against the enemy.

12. *Your enemy can be someone you have placed great trust in.* Those closest to you can change overnight. No one is immune from disloyalty. Everybody is a target to the enemy to destroy your purpose. Continually evaluate those you've placed in trust. My opinion here is, never share everything with everyone around you. People are fickle! Someone you've confided in may become offended with you and then they will have to fight the feeling of exposing you in that hour. Many fail at this point. So remember this when you're in a battle.

13. *Your enemy is anyone who continues to defend the ungodly.* I've seen this and experienced this many times. When a person starts standing up and defending those who

you know are not living for God, there's a reason. Most of the time it's because they've already made some kind of connection to those people. This happens a lot in youth ministry. Peer Pressure is hard to overcome at that age.

14. ***Your enemy is anyone who is comfortable in the presence of the ungodly.*** To be friends with the world is to be at enmity with God.

15. ***Your enemy is anyone who attempts to abort your dreams.*** All you have to experience to abort your dreams is someone saying that it is impossible. Hearing negative words are seeds that infiltrate your mind to weaken the wall of your dreams. Doubt can creep in and cause the foundation of expectation to break and crumble around you. When you reveal your dreams and your visions, notice the first person that becomes a negative voice. They are revealing more than you know.

16. ***Expect an enemy to show up at the birth of any miracle in your life.*** Miracles attract attack. Miracles are dangerous to the enemy's strength and stand. Miracles defeat his morale in the camp. When God starts showing His power, the enemy has to attack. When we are moving in the gifts of miracles, the enemy is moving to discredit us. Satan may not discredit the miracle, but if he can discredit you then he can stop someone else from being set free.

Notice that the Bible does not just warn us about the Devil; we are also warned about <u>people.</u> We have to understand that people can be more dangerous to our lives than demons.

Demons do not destroy ministries; people do. Satan and all his demons have been spiritually defeated by the Blood of Jesus Christ! So the enemy has been conquered. The church has a mandate that no demon or devil will prevail against the church *(Matthew 16:18)*. If Satan can't destroy the church then His only weapon will be to control the church. How is he going accomplish this task? Through people. Many churches have fallen prey to wrong people that have been placed in leadership. I have been in many churches where the deacons, elders and board members believed that the church belonged to them and not to God. I have also seen what can happen when disloyalty is in leadership. Jezebels and Absalom spirits under Satan's control can destroy a church.

It would be beneficial for you to evaluate every relationship you are in right now. Make sure they are increasing you more than they are influencing you to do wrong things. In the end, they will cause you to be defeated. Monitor your conversations with those around you. Listen to them. Do they consistently attack leadership? If they do, move swiftly from them. They're going to cause you to lose God's favor.

When Satan knows you are aware of his tactics, he then moves to finding someone who will get your focus. He'll try to use anyone, your spouse, your children and your parents to break your focus. When someone is breaking your focus, they are now interpreted as your enemy.

CHAPTER FIVE

WARFARE
OVER
FAILURE

"If you can accept your loses you will never win." *Vince Lombardi*

Real winners hate losing more than they love winning. Winners are simply those who are willing to do what losers won't. Winners have routines; losers just do it when they feel like it. Winners possess the one trait the losers don't; they possess the willingness attitude. There is a big difference between wanting to and willing to. Those who are willing always end up on the top of success. Winners wake up every day with a plan. They schedule the night before how they're going to live out their next day. Losers just wake up. *"Success is found under the alarm clock."* Benjamin Franklin

Here's something I've discovered in life. If you don't plan your day, your day will plan you. If you don't plan your life, your life will plan you. This same pattern works with crisis also. Never allow your crisis to command your life. What I mean by that is sometimes you are going to make divine plans in your life and a decision that is going to weaken the enemy's hold on others. When you do, the enemy is going to create a crisis. Why? In hoping you will change your plans due to the crisis. This is when you must discern the enemy and the battle that is engaged in stopping you.

Without a plan you will fail.

I had such an incident not too long ago. I was in Lamar, Texas, preaching for my friend Pastor Walter Hallam. My daughter was pregnant and went into labor while I was there. We were all excited and everything was going as planned. Pastor Walter went on vacation with his family, and I was scheduled to fill his pulpit that evening. My daughter was scheduled to deliver my first grandbaby.

Things changed. ***Crisis hit!*** My daughter's labor lasted way too long and by the next day things had drastically changed. They had to rush her in for a C-section. When they cut her open the stench of infection filled the room. The baby came out with a fever and she was rushed to the NICU. (Neonatal Intensive Care Unit)

I was sitting in my hotel room waiting for my phone to ring and hear the wonderful news about my new grandbaby. When the phone rang, it wasn't the great news I was expecting. My wife explained that my daughter was bleeding internally and my granddaughter was in the **NICU** with fever. After my wife and I finished that conversation, I began to pray for God's touch. Then an hour later, my wife called and said that our daughter was laboring to breathe… then the phone went dead and my mind went crazy. My heart felt like it was about to explode, my mind was tormenting me with all kinds of wrong thoughts. I was pacing the floor, crying and trying to find a flight out of Houston. I wasn't even thinking about seeing my granddaughter. My heart was obsessing over whether I would see my daughter again.

Nothing I was attempting to do was working out. I couldn't find a flight fast enough, and even if I could find a flight I still had to drive an hour to the airport, fly 3 hours to Charlotte and drive an hour to the hospital.

Now, this is where the meaning "don't allow the crisis to change your plans" comes in. Suddenly, in the middle of my crisis, I felt the presence of the Holy Spirit in my hotel room. At the hour when my heart was about to melt with anguish, the Holy Spirit said to me, ***"STOP!*** *You have no control over what's about to happen. By the time you get home, what is going to happen will have happened. Live or die! You have no control, But Son, I do!"*

The next thought that came was this, *"What are you going to do? How are you going to react? Are you going to allow every crisis cause you to melt down? Are you going to allow crisis to change your divine plans, or are you going to keep your plan and trust Me?"*

All of a sudden, faith shot into my spirit. I said it once but I want to say it again, I cannot imagine living life or going through a battle where I could not call on Something bigger than my own intellect.

What do you do when you've run out of answers? What do you do, or whom do you turn to when your crisis has moved beyond the smartest person on the earth? When your daughter's life depends on you having a bigger faith system, one that reaches higher than the doctors and nurses in the room? I put my faith and trust in GOD!

I decided to go on to preach that night and give it over to God. I had a word from GOD burning in my spirit. I walked up to the pulpit and let the Holy Spirit use me. I preached a powerful word. I heard the Holy Spirit say while I was preaching, "IT IS FINISHED... DON'T WORRY... IT'S DONE."

Altars were full. People were lying on the floor crying and worshipping God. After the service, my cell phone buzzed and I saw it was my wife calling. When I answered, she said here someone wants to speak with you. The voice I heard next was my daughter. She said, *"Daddy, I am fine. We are about to eat, all is great, Monroe's (my granddaughter) fever has broken, and she's being released from the NICU."* All of this happened within two hours of obeying God. Now here is where the power hits. The Lord says to me.

"SON, WHEN YOU PURSUE WHAT I'VE CALLED YOU TO PURSUE, I WILL KILL WHAT'S PURSUING YOU!"

I said all that to say this. You are going to experience battles most of your life. Why? Because we are at war! We are going to have to accept this concept. We are called the Army of God. Let me give you some Warfare Strategies...

Strategy One: You must declare war on your enemy.

To fight successfully you're going to have to identify and recognize your enemy. Think about this. Instead of waiting on the enemy to always attack first, why not stand up and declare war! Let the enemy know you're not afraid! When you declare war you now position your posture to fight. The church has taken a passive role in spiritual warfare for too long. This has produced a weak church. Because we have shut ourselves into our four walls, the whole country has gone crazy. I don't blame what's happening in our schools, government or neighborhoods on Satan. I blame it on the believer being too passive. We've made peace where we should've been declaring war.

Strategy Two: Fight the urge to fight the enemy the same way you fought him before.

Don't fight the same way you fought in the last battle. Tactics have changed. Events have changed. You have changed. What worked yesterday may not work today. Your ability to seek fresh instructions from the Holy Spirit is going to keep you ahead of the enemy's plans.

Facts:
1. Drop preconceived notions.
2. Forget the last battle.
3. Keep inventing a new plan.
4. Adapt to current events and times.
5. Re-examine your belief system and your principles.

Strategy Three: In the turmoil of the battle, do not lose your peace of mind.

You have to keep your mind in the middle of major attacks and in terrible battles. It is very important that you guard your mind. Do not allow yourself to become overwhelmed or intimidated by the opposition that has come against you. The greater the enemy the bigger the rewards are.

"Keep thy heart with all diligence; for out of it are the issues of life." Proverbs 4:23

Strategy Four: Create a sense of expectation and urgency.

You fight better when you stay motivated. Expectation is

more important than anyone is telling you. God doesn't move because you want Him to. He doesn't respond because you tell Him or beg Him to. He doesn't move in miracles just because you showed up. Needs do not attract Him.

God moves at the level of your expectation.

Expectation is so powerful. Even the enemy can believe God can. When we say, "I believe God can," we are identifying that we know God is powerful and able. That's not hard to do. After all, God is able. The power is released when you believe God will! Now that's expectation! Believe right now that God will. He will bless me. He will heal me. He will come through in my crisis. Expectation! Work on keeping it alive in your walk, in your warfare and in your life. Just to be clear, let me give you this old quote: *"Expectation is the breeding ground for miracles."*

Strategy Five: Be attentive to details. Avoid the snares.

One of the greatest problems in the life of prosperity and peace is that a spirit of complacency creeps in. It's a dangerous place to be when we become too comfortable. In a season of great prosperity the ability to fight or to engage in conflict fades. That's why Peter told us in I Peter 5:8 to be sober, to be vigilant. *"Be sober, be vigilant; because your adversary the devil walks about like a roaring lion, seeking whom he may devour."* I really like The Message Bible's translation on these verses.

"Keep a cool head. Stay alert. The Devil is poised to pounce, and would like nothing better than to catch you napping. Keep your guard up. You're not the only ones plunged into these hard times. It's the same with Christians all over the world. So keep a firm grip on the faith. The suffering won't last forever. It won't be long before this generous God who has great plans for us in Christ—eternal and glorious plans they are! --- will have you put together and on your feet for good. He gets the last word; yes, he does." I Peter 5:8-11 MSG

11 Steps to a Victorious Life:
1. Keep a cool head.
2. Stay alert.
3. Be conscience that the Devil is poised to pounce.
4. Do not be caught napping.
5. Keep your guard up.
6. You are not alone.
7. Keep a firm grip on your faith.
8. Attack will not last forever.
9. God is generous and has a great plan for us.
10. You will be repaired and restored in the end.
11. God will get the last word over your life.

Strategy Six: Avoid the weakness of thinking like the group.

General Patton was quoted saying. *"If everyone in the room is thinking alike, then someone in the room isn't thinking."*

In this strategy, I'm not advocating not to use and listen to other people. I'm speaking more about not becoming lazy and make sure you do your own thinking. No one will win or succeed alone, but someone has to lead. Someone has to take the reins. Everything rises and falls on leadership. If you're not the lead dog then the scenery never changes. In taking the lead, make sure you don't alienate those who are helping you win the battle.

Helpful Hints:
1. Create a chain of command.
2. Create an atmosphere of unity and camaraderie.
3. Divided leadership is dangerous.
4. Look for those who can fill your voids.
5. Rely on others expertise but don't become captive to them.
6. Make sure you get rapid and correct information from the trenches.
7. Be cautious of those who are politically inclined in your midst.

Strategy Seven: Control Chaos

Remember that order never happens randomly. Calculate disorder. Every unit will experience a break down in advancement. The earth is set up to break down. Everything breaks down. Your job is to keep chaos from happening; to do that you're going to have to exercise order in the midst of chaos. Order dispels chaos. Matter of fact when you see chaos in any area of your life, that's the proof you've failed to exercise order.

Facts:
1. Keep yourself in position to force (Sun Tzu's).
2. Motivate yourself to follow instructions "in spirit, not just by the letter."

Strategy Eight: Choose your battles

Never allow the enemy to decide when you fight. Never let your enemies decide your place of battle. If you're being drawn out to fight make sure you're not being ambushed. If possible, always fight in the high places. It's a better place to be when you're elevated above your enemy. The best way to stay elevated is to keep your heart and mind in praise and worship to God.

You need to know your strengths and weaknesses to pick your place of battle. Know your strengths and lean toward them. The power of warfare is to outlast your enemy and to weaken his energy, resources and morale.

One of the enemy's tactics is deception. His goal will be to make him appear larger and more powerful than you.

Facts:
1. Learn to make do with what you have.
2. Do not rely on what you have only. Rely on your faith.
3. Make sure you don't fight a battle based on your pride.
4. Know your limits.
5. Never fight past what you have in resources.

CHAPTER SIX

WARFARE OVER YOUR MIND

God, I pray protection over my thoughts and over my focuses so that my mind doesn't become persuaded to agree with my crisis or enemy. Dr. G

"If you are going to win any battle, you have to do one thing. "You have to make the mind run the body. Never let the body tell the mind what to do... the body is never tired if the mind is not tired." General George S. Patton

Satan's most frequent and consistent attack is directed against your mind. He sends his hosts out with an arsenal of weapons such as:

1. Lies
2. Threats
3. Intimidation
4. Questions
5. Accusations
6. Lust and other Enticements

These attacks start as early as childhood. Abused children will experience the lie that the abuse was there fault, they deserved it or they are not worth anything to anyone.

As many children are physically developing, questions from the enemy often appear in their thoughts regarding their sexual identity. Over and over these thoughts emerge causing confusion, shame and fear.

Once a child begins to receive any lie as truth, more lies will appear to reinforce the first lie. After a while, the child will begin to focus on their own shortcomings and perceive the rejection of others. Sometimes people are directed by the enemy into children's' lives to prey on them and add more reinforcement to the lies.

When parents do not reflect the character of God to their children, their children can and will project the shortcomings. I heard this quote one day and I believe it applies here. "If parents aren't willing to die for Jesus, our children will not be willing to live for Him." Many will push wrong and religious ideologies on their child's perception of God.

For instance, if one or more parents are cold, lacking in emotion, rigid and constantly preoccupied with other things, the child will see God as lacking compassion, unloving and not there for them. Many have been raised with false expectations and realties of whom and what God is all about.

The enemy encourages these false mindsets. Then the person becomes vulnerable to any word of affirmation, any word of acceptance. They begin to seek out anyone who can make them feel important and needed. Here's the damage; it will not matter if those words come from good or bad sources, as long as they are being said. Not every person encouraging you is an encourager.

We have to reach back into the past and allow the truth of God's word to clean up those areas in our minds that are distorted and causing our present to be distorted and connected to our past when God is trying to connect us to our future.

UNPACK YOUR BAGS BEFORE YOU ENGAGE

Many bring a lot of baggage from their childhood into adulthood. Some grow up in homes where there has been considerable control, manipulation and emotional or physical abuse. Women are often "led" to find a man of similar qualities to continue the destructive, negative reinforcements in their lives. Be very conscientious to the way the enemy wants to destroy you. We cannot underestimate the enemy's influence in any of these situations.

In many cases, the enemy already has claims upon parents and even grandparents. Now the enemy focuses on the children because he knows that the consequences of family sins can make the children vulnerable to similar attacks.

Reveal your mental wound and let the Holy Spirit start unpacking your old baggage. Empty the suitcase; God has another one ready for you. This one is full of joy and peace. Open your mind and let out these false and vain imaginations.

My wife and I pastor counsel people together. We minister to many who have believed the enemy's lies about themselves for years. These lies are strengthened in the strongholds of low self-esteem, self-hatred, poor mental image and a bad self-portrait.

How can these people expect to live a life of faith when their minds have become a corridor of confusion and empty feelings of false imagery? It is very difficult for them, as believers, to live by faith. The enemy continues to beat them with lies and accusations, causing doubt and hopelessness.

We see many adults who are full of anger, bitterness and un-forgiveness all as a result of a weakened mind.

Some time in their life, often in childhood, they have been hurt deeply by someone. The enemy will constantly give them "flashback memories" of that situation. The memories are so painful that they constantly stir up the anger, bitterness and resentment. These emotions can be so strong that it is very difficult for that person to forgive, even though they know the need to.

We could continue indefinitely with these scenarios, but it is my hope you have gotten the point concerning the enemy's activity directed toward your thoughts.

What is a person to do when their mind has been under assault for such a long time? My answer to that is not simple or easy, but we have to start somewhere.

1. It is extremely important to correct the wrong perceptions of God. Any balanced study of the character of God will be extremely beneficial. I cannot emphasize enough how important it is for you to correct your perception of God and have it to line up with the Scriptures. God is not a man!

2. It is equally important to discover what God has to say about you. You need to know your true identity according to the Word of God. The enemy has been distorting and lying about you so that you have a false perception of yourself. We have a simple study available on our website which you can use to discover what the

Word of God says about you. You must know who you are in relation to the God that is in you!

You can never discover the purpose you've been born to do if you lack the truth about who you are. If you can't see the real you, then the enemy will assign others to keep identifying you. You are not a mistake. You are not who people say you are; you are who God says you are!

3. You must take captive your every thought and make it obedient to Christ. The apostle Paul tells us to do this in <u>2 Corinthians 10:5.</u> The first two steps, "Knowing God" and "The Believer's Identity in Christ," are the beginning of that process. It is imperative that you fill your mind with **TRUTH** to counteract the lies you have believed. You also have to confess specifically that you have believed the lies of the enemy and ask God to forgive you and cleanse you.

Part of taking your thoughts captive is to start *disciplining yourself* concerning the things you watch in the movies, TV and the Internet, as well as the things you read in books and magazines. You need to clean up what you are allowing to influence your mind and emotions. The apostle Paul tells us in <u>Philippians 4:8</u>, *"Finally, brethren, whatever things are true, whatever things are noble, whatever things are just, whatever things are pure, whatever things are lovely, whatever things are of good report, if there is any virtue and if there is anything praiseworthy – <u>meditate on these things.</u>"*

It won't be easy at first, but with God's help and a desire to please Him, you can overcome and claim victory.

4. God has given each of us direct access to Himself through prayer. He said that we could come boldly into His presence and present our requests to Him. Most people do not take advantage of this great privilege. Many see it only as an obligation rather than a way to experience fellowship with the Lord.

Why is *Prayer, Praise, and Worship* so under attack in our services?

One of the things I have noticed is that church has turned into speed services. We enter and leave within an hour. Think about this... there is not much else in life that is so rushed through as church services. Even movies are getting longer.

Church is getting shorter and shorter. We meet less and less. It's become Seeker sensitive instead of God sensitive! I was sitting with a friend of mine from Germany who was a minister behind the Iron Curtin. He had to build an underground church. His passion for the church was contagious. The proof you have the Holy Spirit in you is proven by your hunger and desire to be with the church. It doesn't matter whether that church meets on Sunday, Wednesday or any other day. After our talk I wondered, how many who say they have the Holy Spirit have such a hunger and passion for God's house?

Parents want their children to come to them with their concerns. How much more does our God want us to come to Him? Jesus spent much time with his Father when He was on this earth.

Without a consistent prayer life and fellowship with the Lord, you will not experience the victory that you desire. God has given us the Holy Spirit to teach us how to pray. God has given us promises to claim. He has given us tremendous provisions to utilize in our daily lives.

In closing, I want to remind you of another statement by the Apostle Paul.

"Do not be anxious about anything, but in every situation, by prayer and petition, with thanksgiving, present your requests to God. And the peace of God, which transcends all understanding, will guard your hearts and your minds in Christ Jesus." Philippians 4:6-7 NIV

It is my prayer that God will bless you with the determination to conquer the enemy's deceptions. It is the Lord's will for you to be free.

TAKE POSSESSION OF YOUR OWN MIND

I had a pastor friend who went through some real hard times. In short, he lost his ministry… shut down his church… lost his house and moved to another city to get away from all the people he knew. This event in his life drove him to a place where he had lost all his friends.

He survived that season and is back in the ministry now and years later is building a church, doing quite well. What was the deciding factor? He didn't allow his mistakes and losses to rob his mind from still believing he could succeed. When you keep your mind intact you keep your future intact. You must take control of your thoughts in times of battle, warfare and crisis. Where your mind is, is where you are. My mind is the power to my actions. If you don't control your mind, your mind will control you. Your life is not the life you're living; it's actually the life you're thinking.

Change your thinking, and you can change your living.

CHAPTER SEVEN

WARFARE OVER YOUR FAMILY

*"Wherefore I desire that ye faint not at my tribulations for you, which is your glory. For this cause I bow my knees unto the Father of our Lord Jesus Christ, Of **whom the whole family** in heaven and earth is named, That he would grant you, according to the riches of his glory, to be strengthened with might by his Spirit in the inner man ." Ephesians 3:13-16 KJV*

I've heard it said many times, "When the families go, so **goes the church**."

Family is important to God. The first thing God did after He made man was give him a wife. This is God's ultimate focus and wish. That man co-exists in a family. This is revealed in the following scripture:

*"So God created man in his own image, in the image of God created he him; male and female created he them. And God blessed them, **and God said unto them, Be fruitful, and multiply, and replenish the earth, and subdue it: and have dominion** over the fish of the sea, and over the fowl of the air, and over every living thing that moveth upon the earth." Genesis 1:27-28 KJV*

God commanded the man and woman to be fruitful, and to multiply to replenish the earth. This happened through the law of sowing and reaping. Adam sowed his seed that created a life of fruitfulness all around him. This was God's design. Man has the ability to create offspring by sowing his seed into a woman. This is how family is produced.

Man's source of power and greatness should not be hinged on how great he becomes or how much money he generates, but by how much he builds his family.

It is obvious that God wasn't concerned about creating a whole race of people. He was interested in creating one man, giving that man a wife and establishing in his own garden, a family. God's first act on earth with humans was creating a family environment.

Family seems to be important to God. The enemy wants to destroy and pollute anything that is important to God. I believe this is why divorce and abnormal relationships that distort the family are running rampant in this society.

"Blessed is the man whose quiver is full of them. They will not be put to shame when they contend with their opponents in court." Psalms 127:5 NIV

The greatest tragedy in the earth is when a father can't recognize that his greatest accomplishments are not the rewards he gets for the success he has accomplished, but what his children receive when they are grown. The proof of a true father is in his children.

I can tell you the saddest days in my life are when I look back and think of the times I wasn't there for my children when they were young. I was so caught up in my own life and what I wanted. The problem was that I wanted to be anywhere but home with the family. I wanted to be off with my friends playing golf or hanging out; only coming home when necessary. I wanted to be around long enough to maintain my family but not long enough to create memories. I can't remember holding them, changing their diapers, or really spending any time with my children in their early years.

Thank God I woke up and started trying to make amends before it was too late.

~FAMILY IS IMPORTANT~

GOD WANTED TO BE KNOWN AS THE GOD OF FAMILY!

This is very interesting to me. Of all the names that God has, when he described Himself to Abram, God used the name "El-Shaddai" - God Almighty. But after God made a covenant with Abraham, God called Himself the God of Abraham, Isaac and

Jacob.

He wanted to be known as the God of families, or as the God of linage.

God is about connecting to a bloodline.

Satan's number one attack is on marriage and the family.

What is the current divorce rate in America?

FAMILY STARTS WITH MARRIAGE.

It is frequently reported that the divorce rate in America is fifty percent. This data is not accurately correct; however, it is reasonably close. *The Americans for Divorce Reform* estimate that "probably 40, or possibly even 50, percent of marriages will end in divorce if current trends continue." This is a projection.

"50% of all marriages in America end in divorce." However, this statement about the divorce rate in America hides all of the details about distribution.

The divorce rate in America for first marriage, versus the second or third marriage, according to Jennifer Baker of the Forest Institute of Professional Psychology in Springfield, Missouri, is as follows:

- 41% of first marriages end in divorce.
- 60% of second marriages end in divorce.
- 73% of third marriages end in divorce.

Divorce is high and it seems that no one is immune from its web. Even men and women of God are falling for this trap. We need to know that God isn't about us saving the world. Jesus didn't even try to save the world. He just worked on twelve men. It's not God's ordained plan for us to reach into the lives of others while reaching past our spouse and children.

I heard a preacher's kid say to me with tears in his eyes, "My dad would treat the other kids in our church better than he treated me. They would get the gifts and the candy first. If there was any leftover then I could have some. I remember more than once leaving upset and hurt because there wasn't any left for me."

This is not how God wanted it to be. I am not trading my wife and kids off to save someone I've never met and may never meet. It was my desire to be a father that was always around the family. I made up my mind that I would be home, I would be at their games, I would watch them grow up and give them memories that dad was always there. I know I was not a perfect dad, but I was not a bad dad either.

Single Parent Homes Are An Epidemic

Single parent family households have become a common occurrence in the United States, and the number of these types of households has been on the rise for the last several decades. Currently in the United States, according to single parent family statistics, there are over 13 million single parents.

A female heads nearly 85 percent of these single parent households while a male heads the remaining households. The vast majority of both female and male single parent households are either divorced or separated. Approximately one-third of female single parents have never been married and less than a quarter of female single parents are remarried. Almost a quarter of single parent fathers remarried, while only about 18 percent of single fathers have never been married. Approximately 1 percent of single parents, both men and women, find themselves single parents as the result of the death of a spouse.

According to single parent family statistics, even though the majority of mothers work full time jobs, almost a third of these families live in poverty and approximately the same percentage receive public assistance.

According to statistics, approximately 11 percent of single fathers live in poverty. In essence, about three times more single parent females live in poverty than their single male parent counterparts.

These reasons can be explained by a number of factors, one being the discrepancy in pay between men and women in the workforce. Income is certainly not the only obstacle faced by single parent families but it may be one of the most stressful and challenging obstacles. This is why I recommend going to a church that believes in teaching on biblical prosperity. Without the Favor of God in your life you will be forced to live a life of lack and struggle. God has set up a system through Kingdom Living for increase.

CHAPTER EIGHT

WARFARE
OVER YOUR MONEY

M

oney is more important than people are telling us.

1. Money is not a miracle.
2. Money is not a mystery.
3. Money doesn't grow on trees.
4. God doesn't send you money.

Money does not follow you; money is waiting on you to show up where you have been assigned to be.

I have been saved and in church for some time now, and I wish someone would have taught me a long time ago the spiritual and scriptural truth about finances.

Let me share a little of my financial past. First of all, my early years have always been a financial struggle. Lack was the norm. I know what it feels like to drive a car that you had to work your faith every time you sat in it. Your faith was, *"Oh God! I hope this car cranks."* There were feelings of worry every time we took a trip that it would break down on the way. I also have the experience that when the car broke down there was never enough in the financial budget to fix it properly.

Besides car depression, I also experienced lack in clothing, lack in paying house bills, medical bills and school debts. The only recourse we had at the time was to file bankruptcy. That also is a journey I had to take. After you go through bankruptcy, you have ten years of cleaning up your past.

Praise God, in the end I learned many things. I began to study the word of God and found out that God wants, and expects, us to be good stewards of what He has given us. Today, I have a great credit score, drive nice cars and live in a nice house.

With that in mind, I want you to know that I do understand financial stress and loss.

WHAT I STAND FOR:
Someone once asked me what we preach and teach at the Favor Center Church. At the time, I really couldn't put into words what I believe. So I talked 'around' what I really wanted to say. Today, I would answer with a little more boldness. We preach and teach Biblical economics. What are Biblical economics? Well, some would call it the prosperity message... others would call it "name it and claim it." I call it **the GOSPEL!**

THREE THINGS THE CROSS TOOK CARE OF:

1. SIN: The cross was the penalty for sin. God accepted Jesus as the last and final sacrifice for the penalty of sin. This gives us access to God through Christ Jesus to be saved and forgiven.

2. SICKNESS: Jesus suffered an extreme beating on His back for the redeeming of our physical bodies. Healing became the right of every believer. We can stand for, and stand in, the healing power of Jesus over every sickness and disease. Our faith in those stripes gives us power over sickness.

3. POVERTY: The only cure for poverty is prosperity. There is no other cure. There is no cure for lack if you do not attach prosperity to the equation. We have to have more than enough to help others.

We have bought into this ideology that only a few can have more and the rest of us have to accept our lives. I say, "NO WAY!" What one man can do, another can do! God is not going to allow only a few to experience financial freedom as the rest suffer. That is not Truth!

This is exactly where the enemy wants you to be. It doesn't matter if you get saved and are ready for Heaven; if you don't have any influence you will take very few with you. This is one of the enemy's greatest warfare; to keep the average Christian in the persuasion that they can never be financially free.

I heard someone once say that prosperity should have been one of the laws or tenants of faith. How would things be different if **Financial Prosperity** would have been added when our fathers were writing the tenants of faith in the doctrinal laws of the protestant church? Imagine how different the church would be right now if we had been persuaded to believe in a prosperity gospel. I believe less people would be broke, busted and living in lack. We sure wouldn't have bought into accepting a life of mediocrity.

The best thing you can do for the poor is, don't become one of them.

We have to win the warfare over money. Without money we have no influence. Money is power! Money is not evil. I am so sick of hearing the ignorant say that God doesn't want us to have money. That is so ridiculous! How stupid does that sound to you? There's a passage in the Bible that says, 'if we know how to give good gifts, being evil; how much more does our Heavenly Father want to give us, for He is perfect (Luke 11:13 paraphrase). We have no control over certain situations without money. Some things can't be prayed for; they have to be paid for. Prayer can't buy property, or build schools or help starving families. Money does that.

I heard someone say "Money won't make you happy." I can testify it won't make you sad either. Money is not everything, true; but it sure helps get most things. I have seen the stress the lack of money puts on people. I've watched marriages fall apart - not because they didn't love each other - but because the lack of finances tore them apart. How does this happen? The stress of debt, the stress of loss and the stress of lack are heavy burdens to carry.

Men and women work painful hours every day to earn money. They give up the most precious time of the day for the entry of money. What angers me is to go to church and never hear leadership teach and preach on God's will for prosperity.

Imagine a father standing in front of his children. He has four kids, 2 boys and 2 girls. The father looks at them and says,

"Children, one of you will be rich, the other will be well off, the other one will barely make it and the last will live in poverty. That is my will... the children that are broke need to live life being grateful that I allow them to live."

Come on! Do you believe he would be considered a great father? NO!

This is exactly the kind of father many churches portray God to be. The truth is that good father's desire for all of their children to be prosperous. They will do all that is within their power to make sure that happens. Now, does that mean every child will? Of course not; but they all have the same potential. The children, not the father, decide the difference.

Get this in your spirit. You need to have more money. Get this in your heart; you're going to have more money.

Why does God want you to have more money?
1. To serve as an example.
2. To give you influence.
3. So you can provide for your family.
4. To carry out the 'great commission.'
   Without money, how would missionaries do their ministries? How would preachers build churches? How could we feed the hungry? This all requires money!
5. To ease the suffering of others.
6. To be a blessing.

"The only people who claim that money isn't important are people who have enough money - so that they are relieved of the burden of thinking about it..." Joyce Carol Oates

MORE IS GODLY

What? Yes! The desire to want more is God given. God made you for increase, not decrease. God manufactured you to sow, to reap, to learn, to grow, to become wiser today than you were yesterday.

The voice that speaks against us having more is an adversarial voice against the Gospel. Gospel means the good news. The gospel is more than just salvation to make Heaven. The gospel is that all three curses are defeated. Poverty, sickness and sin have lost their power! Christ redeemed us from them so we need to claim our deliverance and walk free from all three.

Anyone who says money won't make you happy-hasn't had any! This is one of the most ridiculous statements I have ever heard. Money may not make you happy, but it won't make you sad. I've been on both sides of this game. I've been in life without money, and I've been in it with money. All I can say is crisis are much easier to get through when you have some money. Sure, I hate for things to break down. Flat tires are frustrating, but I guarantee you it's more frustrating to have a flat tire with no money to fix it.

Remember this. Money is a tool. That's all it is. It's a tool to be used. Money is an amplifier. Whatever money touches, grows. Give money to a drug addict and he becomes a better drug addict. Money didn't make him a drug addict; it just amplified what he was.

Debt is killing the USA.

Debt is not the will of God. Debt has never been God's way. Debt is an attempt to have more and do more before your time. Debt is a system that hell has invented to keep people in bondage to a prison of earning enough money just to pay their debt and never have enough to be free. **Debt is a choice.**

I've witnessed in my own life as well as many others that one bad decision in your past sets up a system of debt. Many people think the answer to getting out of debt is work and chase money. Money is the answer to debt for sure, but God never intended for us to spend a lifetime chasing money. When you find yourself in the system of earning a living and chasing money to sustain the debt hole you have created, you now become a part of the system you can't find your way out of.

What do most do in this situation? They try to use debt to

get out of debt. This doesn't work. This will never work. You can't use the enemy's system to free yourself from his bondage. You're not designed to earn anything. You're designed by God to live a life, not earn one.

"I have come that you might have life, and that you might have a more abundant life," John 10:10 the words of Jesus. (*Paraphrased*)

"[Credit is a system whereby] a person who can't pay gets another person who can't pay, to guarantee that he can pay." — *Charles Dickens*

Unfortunately, debt is not the problem. Debt is a symptom of the problem. The problem can be broken into five things:

1. **Poor money management.**
2. **Spending before you can afford to spend.**
3. **The lack of patience.**
4. **The lack of self-control (which is part of the fruit of the spirit).**
5. **When want is stronger than need.**

God is very concerned about money. There are over 2,000 scriptures that deal with money. God spoke more about finances than He did Heaven and hell.

Reasons for debt:

1. **Lack of knowledge**... Ignorance is a curse. God made provision for ignorance. Read Numbers 15:24-29. What is ignorance? It is the refusal to learn.

   It's not what you know that's costing you; it's what you don't know!

2. **Covetousness**... It is dangerous to covet and want what others have. You can become so consumed by what they

have and what you do not have, that you begin to lose sight of what you could have. Another way of looking at the sin of covetousness is comparison. You will always compare their strengths against your weakness; what you have against what you lack. You will always lose when you compare your life to others.

3. **Greed...** What is Greed? It is taking all that one can get with no thought of others and their needs. Greed is when you hold on to what you have so tightly that what you have now has you. Lucifer steals, man hoards and God gives. The only cure for greed is giving. You can't pray greed out of your house. You can sow your way out of greed.

4. **Disobedience...** So many are living in debt and loss simply because they refused Godly instruction. Disobedience is very costly and dangerous. Reward is always scheduled on the other side of obedience. The difference between lack and prosperity, sickness and healing, problems and promotion, is an obeyed instruction. I've heard this quote a number of times. *"The instruction you are willing to follow creates the future you are able to walk in." Dr. Mike Murdock*

POVERTY IS A CHOICE

You read that right. I said it. People who live in lack and poverty decided to live that way. According to Deuteronomy 30, prosperity is a choice. If prosperity is a choice then poverty must be also.

Deuteronomy 28:11 tells us that prosperity is granted by the Lord. Ephesians 3:20 says that prosperity is the fruit of God's favor. According to Matthew 25:25-30, God expects us to walk in prosperity and increase. For us to have Biblical prosperity we must have the true meaning to prosperity. Prosperity is to have enough

THE VOICE OF PROSPERITY

The prosperous have a different way of speaking than those who walk in lack and poverty. You must stop the voice of lack to have the voice of prosperity. The voice of lack says things like, *"I'm broke... I'm never going to have that... I wish I could."*

You can! Stop thinking and speaking that you can't. You can! You can have anything, do anything and be anything you want to be with God on your side. If one man can do it, another man can do it.

Refuse to have conversation that sounds like you are a victim. Victim conversation does only one thing. It keeps you a victim. Stop complaining about your problem, your life, your pain, your hurts, your past and your mistakes. Start working the law of grace. God has given you all you need, and it is in the power of the tongue.

God set me free one afternoon. I was talking to God and asking Him where my blessing was. God's spirit spoke into my spirit these words *"Son, as long as you keep your focus and faith on an external power, you will never walk in blessings and increase."*

Blessings are not coming to you... they are coming from within you.

The blessings are not coming to you. When I say blessings, I mean all of them - money, health, favor and the things you want and need. These things aren't out in your future; they are already in your present. **They are in you!** They live in your faith. The sooner you realize that God has placed in you everything you need to obtain anything you want, the quicker you are going to walk in favor. In Jesus, we live. In Jesus, we move. In Him we have our being. He's in me, and I am in Him. Together, we are moving to fulfill the purpose and assignment for the Kingdom's advancements.

The difference between failure and favor is YOU!

Isaiah 42 says, *they that wait on the Lord get renewed strength.* That's awesome, but that's not New Testament. They had to wait on the Lord in the old days. That means they had to wait for Him to show up. God didn't exist in them, He was moving around them. I'm not saying that God couldn't live in them but that He chose not to live in them. So, they had to wait on God to appear, or show up. Then they could walk in the power and in the blessings. Then they could experience His miracles; but we live in another era. They lived life before the cross; we live life after the cross. They had the God around them *(before the cross.)* We are walking with God in us *(life after the cross).* We are New Testament believers. We have been set free from the old era. We have become the temple that God lives in. God isn't in some faraway place waiting on us to call for Him to come. No sir! He's right here in us.

New Testament believers should read it this way. ***Those who wait in the Lord shall have greater strength.*** I'm not waiting on God. God has already done what He's going to do. What I am doing is **waiting in Him**.

When we say God around me, we are referencing that He has covered me. When we say God is in me, we are referencing that God dwells on the inside of me. Old Testament God became the God that covers *(Genesis 3:21).* The New Testament God is the God that freed us. We no longer need covering because we've been freed and cleansed through the blood of Jesus Christ. In the Old Testament, understand that they could only have God who would show up at certain times. They had to wait for God before they could experience a miracle or a victory. We can experience the miracles of God immediately through His Son Jesus Christ who abides in us. We have immediate access to the very throne of Grace by which we can come every day with boldness! *(Hebrew 4:16)*

CHAPTER NINE

WARFARE OVER
YOUR
CONVERSATIONS

Many are living out a conversation they had in their past. Most people have no idea how powerful their words are. It is important to understand that by our words we are exalted and by our words we are defeated. They say that children who are abused physically can heal easier that those children that were abused verbally. Words never die.

4 ACTIONS THAT REVEALS US:

1. Your Mouth
2. Your Movement
3. Your Money
4. Your Moods

The greatest thing you can learn about warfare is that your greatest asset is also your greatest liability. Your mouth is a powerful tool; with it you can speak life to a thing or death to a thing.

"Death and life are in the power of the tongue, And those who love it will eat its fruit." Proverbs 18:21

In this verse, you see that it says that those who love it will eat the fruit of your words. Your conversation is more powerful than you will ever know. If you can master your conversation you can master your future. We are living today the conversation we had yesterday. Your words are in constant battle over your life. Your mind decides your mouth's expression.

The truth is that we are *"feeling beings."*

We are moved and led, most of the time, by how we feel. Feelings are powerful. Don't let anyone tell you that your feelings aren't real. They are real. However, no matter how real they are to you, it doesn't mean they are based on truth.

What you are feeling is actually the truth in what you perceive. A wife can feel like her husband doesn't care about her. Now, that feeling is real to her, but that doesn't mean that her husband doesn't care. In reality, he does care. He does love her; he just doesn't know how to demonstrate it in a way his wife receives it and ultimately feels it.

There are five senses that produce feelings:
1. Skin. We feel through touch.
2. Eyes. What we see can decide feelings.
3. Nose. Smell can have a powerful effect on our feelings.
4. Ears. Hearing is a powerful mood changer!
5. Mouth. Words create atmosphere. Words can decide feelings.

Our words create powerful feelings of victory or defeat. As a matter of fact, my words and my thoughts have no power without feelings.

Feelings are your truth, but not necessarily the TRUTH.

Master your feelings and you can master your words and environment. The power of feelings is so under estimated in the church. I get so irritated when someone says feelings aren't real. **Feelings are real;** they just may not be telling you the truth. Your feelings are being fed by your emotions, your emotions are being fed by your thoughts, and your thoughts are giving your feelings validity through your words. So, if I can master my thoughts then I can master my emotions. If I can master my emotions then I will in truth master my words, which form my conversations. The better your feelings are, the better your conversations become and the better your days will be. Take stock in your moods and feelings for there is an unbroken connection between your feelings and your visible world!

Feelings are the fuel for your environment.

WORDS REALLY DO MATTER

Words really do matter. Words are the most powerful weapon you can have to combat negative information. We motivate with words. We encourage or discourage with words. We are justified with words. We are condemned with words. We can create feelings so strong with words that men will charge an enemy shooting at them. Battles are won and lost from the power of words. The Bible is written with words. God called His Son the Word. John 1:1 says, ***"In the beginning was the Word, and the Word was with God, and the Word was God."***

Words are not cheap. We may have cheapened them in our thinking but when they leave our lips they become eternal. Words define us. Words interpret us. Interpretation is not cheap so therefore words are never cheap. Words are "Doors, Walls and Bridges!"

Could our words have created wounds in someone? Could your words be destroying your harvest instead of protecting it? Could your words have been the seed for your harvest? Could it be that you are living the words spoken over you as a child?

I have a friend who showed me something about the woman with the issue of blood. You can find this story in Luke 8:43-48. This woman had an issue of bleeding for twelve years. The Bible says that she spent all that she had and grew worse. In this same passage we see a man whose 12 year old daughter was sick. Could it be that God was trying to reveal to us that our issues as adults could've been decided when we were children? WOW!

Have we picked up wrong conversation through our childhood; using words that are negative, derogatory and hurtful because that is what we heard as children? We must be willing to fight the warfare of words. It's time to win the battle of words.

We could be living in a prison in life that our words have created. Think for a moment! How do you speak to your spouse? How do you speak to your children? How do you speak to your coworkers? How do you speak to others? Do your words edify and uplift or are they spoken in anger and hate.

One more thought before we move on. God gave you two eyes, two ears and one mouth. It is obvious to me that God wanted us to spend twice as much time seeing and hearing than speaking. The reason? Words are powerful! We must win the warfare over our conversations.

CHAPTER TEN

WARFARE OVER YOUR MOMENTUM

*M*otion is relative to perception! Just because you don't see yourself moving doesn't necessarily mean you're not moving. If you were traveling at the speed of sixty miles per hour in a car on the interstate, you could look out the window and see the trees and signs passing you with great swiftness. That would give you the perception that you're moving down the highway. However, let's say you're reading a book in your lap while moving at 60mph. The book appears to be still which gives you the perception that you are not moving.

If I were standing on the overpass looking down at the oncoming cars, I would see you and all the contents of the car moving at the same speed. This is the law of motion; motion is relative to perception. This is very important to understanding momentum.

When you feel like you're not going anywhere or that nothing is happening or changing, that may not be reality! It may just be your perception.

God is sitting on the over pass of our lives. He's observing something in our lives much greater than you and I can observe. We feel like our life is going nowhere, and we are doing nothing. God always has a higher perception than man. God sees us moving faster than our perception is revealing to us. Even when we feel like all blessings have stopped, that's when we must understand that our perception could be deceiving us. Perception is defined as, *"the way you think about or understand someone or something; the ability to understand or notice something; the way that you notice or understand something using one of your sense."*

Perception is your awareness, discernment, observation and sensitivity. These are very important in understanding the power of movement and momentum. Motion is relative to your awareness, to your ability to discern, and the observation and sensitivity to know that God is doing something even in your stillness season.

Motion Decides Emotions

How important is movement? It's more important than most believe or understand. When someone is experiencing depression, the first thing they tend to do is to stop all activities. Think of the times you felt depressed or discouraged. What did you want to do? Absolutely nothing. I can remember times when I was down; I would sit around sighing and moping. I didn't have energy to do or try anything new. All I wanted to do was sit on the couch or lay in my bed. The sense of all actions cease for a time. The truth is that what we need to do is get up and get moving. Motion decides emotions. Take a walk. Go to the gym. Start a project. When you start moving your mind will start healing. We were created for movement. One of the reasons the Bible says we should be still and know that He is God is because deciding to stay still is a sacrifice to the true make up of mankind. We were born to move.

Movement does not mean you have momentum

One of the greatest deceptions in life is to believe that movement is ***momentum.*** This deceives many; they believe that if they're moving they're making progress and succeeding. This is sad because they are putting efforts where there is no productivity.

I have witnessed so many people moving, looking busy but never getting anywhere. They move to the altar but stay the same. They move to and from new jobs, but they're always in the same financial crisis. I've watched people move from one relationship to another but are never happy. Movement means nothing if while you're moving you make no progress.

Movement without arrival is maddening

Movement without productivity is exhausting. It is nothing more than driving on an endless highway and arriving nowhere. Movement without purpose and destiny is like driving in a cul-de-sac around and around, going one way. No matter how long you drive, nothing changes and there is no way out. You're going to have to be willing to do 3 things if you want to stop the craziness of continuous movement to nowhere.

1. *Stop for a season.*

2. *Observe your present situation.*
3. *Be willing to regress to progress.* You're going to have to go down the same road to get out of the cul-de-sac.

So many people in our churches assume they are creating spiritual momentum because they go to church and read their Bible. They are not. My wife is our Praise and Worship leader and says all the time, *"You're not a worshipper because you came to church; you're a worshipper when you worship."* Many have deceived themselves into a persuasion that if I show up that's enough. It is not! Just because you made movement doesn't mean you have momentum. Sadly, movement is not momentum. You're going to have to set some standards and make some changes to start creating momentum in your life.

You have to understand what causes momentum. The force behind you is stronger than the opposition that is attempting to hold you in place. Momentum is a force that is pushing you; not pulling you. Momentum is the power behind movement.

A ship in full motion has such momentum that if you cut off all power the ship will still move one mile before it stops. Why? It has momentum behind it; a force stronger that the opposition in front of it attempting to stop it. That opposition takes one mile to affect the forward movement of the ship.

This is why Satan hates to see believers who have momentum. Even when they seem to have lost power, they still are experiencing tremendous breakthroughs.

Prepare for a momentum to shift.

Momentum has more power when the movement of an object has density.

Your momentum is shifting in your favor. The heavier the object, the more momentum that is created. For instance, I can throw a towel at a brick wall, but the towel lacks the weight necessary to create the momentum necessary to experience a break through, no matter how hard and fast I throw it. Weight decides the potential of momentum.

The valley you've conquered creates powerful momentum.

Momentum is created when you win in the valley. When you come out of the lowest places of your life a winner, you create such momentum that the rest of the enemy's opposition is easily beaten. The force behind you is now greater than the opposition that is in front of you.

What can you say to Jesus today to threaten him? When you have survived death's final blow and rise from the ashes of the grave, the enemy has no more power to threaten you. One of the ways Satan stops momentum is to build a crisis in front of you that is so great, you will not even attempt to enter into conflict or fight back. Jesus knew the devastation of the cross. He didn't see the crisis but the joy of living after the crisis was defeated. Jesus used the eyes of revelation and kept them more focused on victory, not the pain of the valley.

*"Looking unto Jesus the author and finisher of our faith; **who for the joy that was set before him endured the cross, despising the shame, and is set down at the right hand of the throne of God."*** Hebrews 12:2 KJV

We must win the warfare over momentum, understanding that God's force is pushing us. We're not being pulled by our destiny; we're being pushed by God's purpose and assignment. The force that is pushing us is now in conflict to the opposition that is attempting to hinder us. The warfare is the decision to stay connected to the force pushing you - your faith - instead of the opposition that is attacking you - your situation.

Don't allow your situation to define you.

When you're facing a situation you have to maintain your faith no matter what. Satan is going to use anything he can to persuade you not to believe in your future. His whole warfare tactic is to scare you bad enough to not even attempt to enter the battle.

Anything Uncontested will flourish.

This is Satan's greatest warfare against believers. All he has to do is put a mountain in front of our lives, a situation that looks so large and intimidating that we immediately lose our focus, passion and become persuaded that there's no use. There's no way we can overcome, overpower or even at best make a dent into the crisis. I have a prophecy for you today. You're going to have to receive this prophecy to succeed in the Kingdom. **Warfare is your destiny.**

The situation isn't going to let up on you if you don't fight; it's going to get bigger and worse. *Anything uncontested flourishes…*

The first thing we do as humans when we are facing situations that are huge and overwhelming is talk about the problem. We spend much time and effort discussing what we are going through. We tell our friends, our family and some people even discuss it with strangers. We are growing the situation in our minds when we talk about it. Our continuous conversation about the problem makes the problem become unconquerable. Our ears are hearing our own words of defeat and those words are defeating us.

The mind will buy into our own discussions. We must fight the urge to talk about the situation! We have to start putting words to our faith. So many people spend countless hours and days discussing their problems with family, friends and coworkers that the situation doesn't get solved, it gets bigger. Why does it get bigger? The words they are speaking are giving it the power of control over their minds and feelings.

I don't care what people say. *Feelings are powerful.* Feelings can be hard to overcome. We may not ever get out of the situation if we can't change the way we feel. It is so important that we look past the situation into our faith and future. You must remind yourself of the word that God has spoken into your heart; the promise that He made to you that proves your situation isn't supposed to destroy you.

You have been anointed for this! Don't let the situation in one season define your feelings. Fight the temptation to allow the loss, the pain and the mountain you are facing to create words of agreement to it.

*"For verily I say unto you, That whosoever **shall say unto this mountain**, Be thou removed, and be thou cast into the sea; and **shall not doubt in his heart, but shall believe that those things which he saith shall come to pass**; he shall have whatsoever he **saith**. Therefore I say unto you, What things so ever ye desire, when ye pray, believe that ye receive them, and ye shall have them.* " Mark 11: 23, 24 KJV

Momentum is a major key in winning in life. When a business has momentum it does bigger things. In sports, momentum shifts are major in determining the outcome of a game. Usually the winner won because they were able to maintain or create momentum. A leader in momentum looks greater than he really is, and a great leader without momentum looks lesser than he really is. Momentum is the key to a powerful life. Work on movement with faith. Let faith push you and destiny pull you. Together, I promise, you will succeed.

13 Momentum Shifters:

1. Praise
2. Worship
3. Word of God
4. God
5. Faith
6. Feelings
7. Occupation
8. Commitment
9. Made up mind
10. Right behavior
11. Warfare
12. Willingness
13. Seed

CHAPTER ELEVEN

WARFARE OVER YOUR CHANGE

T here are really only two types of people; those who accept the need for change and those who don't. People who change will grow and become productive in their lives; those who don't will stay trapped and imprisoned to their present. They become stagnate and never fulfill their divine purpose.

The easiest way to live life is in the status quo and comfort zone of non-changers.

Many have this ideology, *"I don't want anything to change around here; I just want things to get better..."* This is where the problem is. You cannot have things better if you cannot allow things to change. The waves of change are constantly crashing on the shores of our daily lives. We must win the warfare over change to have a successful and winning life.

- Change comes in all sizes in life.
- Change comes at all stages of life.
- The real question is, can people really change?

Change never happens swiftly

Understand this law. Change is never swift especially when it comes to changing your thought life, habits and momentum. Many never change because they're unwilling to pay the price of time for change to manifest. That's why the Bible says that those who can wait on the Lord always have renewed strength. Waiters are winners when it comes to change. Maybe I should put it this way. Patience is the key to lasting change. Be willing to do without, be alone and to even be frustrated. Change happens in four stages.

1. *First stage*: <u>Letting Go Stage:</u> This is the place where you have to let wrong things go. Wrong thinking! Wrong ideas! Wrong habits and wrong friends! At this stage, you must

decide and be *persuaded* that you need to change. This is the easiest part of change. Make up your mind right now that you need to change. It's better if you can use the Holy Spirit to help you see what needs to change. We call the need to change in the church "conviction." Conviction isn't thought about much anymore. Most modern day churches are afraid of conviction. The leadership is in fear of losing their congregation when they start to feel convicted. I assure you, conviction is the most powerful feeling for change. Letting go is easier than walking away.

"If you can't be convicted you can't be converted." Dr. Grillo

2. *Second Stage:* **Coming Out Stage**: Here's where you will be challenged. Nothing in this stage makes any sense. You will be mentally tormented. You will be full of anxiety and a weird feeling comes over you. The excitement of stage one is over. Now, the battle to let go begins. This battle is real. Here's where you can activate the power of Jesus at work in your life if you have accepted Him as your Savior. You can use the power of the Holy Spirit to help comfort and calm you in the coming out stage. You have to depart from your old season if you desire to enter a new season.

3. *Third Stage*: **Transition Stage**: This stage takes more time. Here's where the warfare begins to really happen. At this point, you've journeyed a while in your coming out stage. Usually, it's at the half way mark when the enemy is going to pour it on. You are now half way to a new you. You are half way between your ***history*** and ***your future.*** Picture yourself sitting in a hallway in this stage. The door behind you has been shut and locked. The door in front of you hasn't opened yet. Now what do you do? You have to wait. You have to grow. This is where you're training your mind to adapt and live in your new season. It's at this stage you have to keep purpose alive.

Where purpose is not known, abuse is inevitable.
This is not a bad place to be. I know what it feels like. It feels like everything around you has died. The truth is that they have. You are now in winter. Winter is the time where everything dies; but plants and trees do not panic in winter. They know all the sap of life has now moved from the branches to the roots. What do the plants and trees know? They know that this season isn't going to last forever. Winter precedes spring. Just like the trees and plants, you have to posture yourself in the transition stage to wait. Worship, praise and study in your waiting. Build an expectation. Why? Because spring is coming and when it comes you will begin to see new things, new growths and new life.

4. *Stage Four*: **The Entering Stage**: Now you have changed. You are now entering what you've been praying for, believing for and waiting for. Your new season, where the old is gone, has arrived. This is the victory stage. You have changed. You are no longer the person you were. You use to be bitter; now you're better. You use to be an addict; now you're free. You use to be overweight; but now you're healthy. You use to be broke; but now you're prosperous. What you use to be attracted to, you are now appalled by. My friend you have changed.

People rarely change. When they do, they usually don't change much. This has been my experience.

Moving into the season of the unusual

Be careful; if you ask God to free you, He's going to move you into a season and a place of the unusual. You better prepare for war when God's ready to take you to a new season. You will have to move through the land of the unpredictable when you begin to move. Here's where the battle rages. Your senses are off. Your mind is stretching to understand. Your feelings are full of fear and reservations.

Nothing Changes without Confrontation

Anything uncontested will flourish. If you're not willing to face and confront certain issues your present has just became permanent. When you're unwilling to face certain issues such as your past or mistakes, you end up stopping the process for change. Anything you're unwilling to confront has proven that it has already conquered your mind. You're momentum has just stopped.

- The proof you belong in your future is your willingness to fight for it.
- The proof of your persuasion is the willingness to confront a thing.
- The proof your faith is larger than your fear is the willingness to confront.

If you refuse to confront an issue, you just made your mind up to stop advancing.

Confrontation for change doesn't necessarily mean you have to argue with someone. You don't have to get into debate; you do have to move toward your enemy. The willingness to enter the environment of an enemy is the power for change. An enemy is anything or anyone who's attempting to stop your change.

What usually causes conflict? When you become larger than your present season. Your present season can no longer sustain your desires, your hungers and your dreams to move forward. You're going to have to confront it. I know I've already written on this but let me say it again. *You can't change your world, if you can't change your conversation.* Make sure you check and double-check what you say and how you say it.

Six things that kept the children of Israel stuck in an unchangeable season:

1. Their lust
2. Tempting God in the wilderness
3. Fornication
4. Their complaining
5. Their unwillingness to believe
6. Fear: They feared the enemies of Canaan.

The circle of change

All of us have to be willing to enter the circle of change. Most of us wouldn't have ever changed without a defining moment. What is a defining moment? It is a moment when you have been defined for your next season.

You will know this moment by four things:
1. Your convictions change.
2. Your encounters change.
3. Your desires change.
4. Your hungers change.

When you begin to see these changes taking place, you have entered a 'Kairos' moment. We must understand that no one changes overnight. Time is not our enemy; it is actually working for us, not against us. We live in and will never stop living in time. The one thing I have learned about time is that it is not prejudiced. It doesn't wait on anyone. You can't stop it. You can't control it. You can't change it. You can only not waste it. We live in what is known as chronological time; time that is measured by seconds, minutes and hours. We can't have an hour without living through minutes, and we can't experience a minute without living through seconds. Everything we do moves through this sequence. This is human time, but that's not GOD! God doesn't live in time nor is He bound to time.

God is beyond time. Time doesn't control God because God is the originator of time. God created time for man. Why? So that man could always be assured that there is a beginning and an end to anything. Seasons wouldn't happen without time. A

"**Kairos**" moment is when God decides to enter time...a God moment. This is the window where **miracles** happen.

Followers of Jesus are challenged to change continually. WE call this maturity or growing to full maturity. Make up your mind today that you're going to allow the Holy Spirit the power to help you change. Change doesn't happen in private. It's decided in private, but the proof of change has to be witnessed by others. You're not better because you say you're better. You are better when others say you've changed.

The proof of God's presence is change.

I have heard hundreds if not thousands say after a Sunday service, *"Man God was here today..."* However, those people who say that have not made any significant change. So my question is this, did God really show up? I believe that what we call God's presence is nothing more than the emotions we feel in the atmosphere of energized praise. When God really shows up, the first things you and I are going to want to do is change and repent.

We realize in God's presence that we are unholy and that we don't and won't ever measure up to His power and His radiance. The proof of God's presence is not shouting or the urge to dance. It isn't the goose pimples that you felt on your arms. The proof of God's presence is CHANGE!

How Can We Change?

Humans are like stones. We resist change by instinct. Resistance to change forces us to test the need for change. Obstinate resistance needs to be overcome because it will get in the way of change. Seek out someone you can talk to about your fears if you are afraid to reveal your deepest insecurities in order to change. Exposure is the first step toward embracing change. Let me close this chapter with some helpful tips on making the change process work for you. Keep these steps in mind when change is upon you.

1. **We can only be change agents if we have embraced change for ourselves.** We must be committed to the process of change.

2. **All change follows a definable sequence of stages.**
   a. First is **Denial**... we refuse to accept we need change.
   b. Second is **Resistance**...we see the need but resist it.
   c. Third is **Exploration**...we check out the new state of affairs.
   d. Final is **Commitment**...we are reconciled to the changes and live at peace with them.

3. **Discipline yourself to become knowledgeable about the change that is happening to you.** Study when you are deciding to change. Find out all you can about the area in which you are changing. If change is being forced on you - such as someone divorcing you or attacking you - find others who have been where you are and survived. Ask them questions. Knowledge is a weapon to facilitate change. Become a fanatical learner.

4. **Be prepared for a lot of reversals and disappointments.** Unfortunately, change is not a linear process. It comes in spurts and takes back as much as it delivers. Also, you cannot always recognize the moment of change when it is happening because sometimes change comes in painful times.

5. **Our greatest opportunities for positive change are to be found in times of apparent failures and disappointments.** In God's eternal plan there is no such thing as failure - **only forced growth.** We are never failures in the Kingdom. If we fail we learn; if we learn then failure is the step to winning. God didn't cause bad things to happen to us, but God always uses them to fulfill his work of grace in us.

6. **Never attempt any change without leaning heavily on the resources of God's provisions.** Humanistic models for change have never been very effective. *"The power of Grace flows most fully when human will chooses to act in harmony with divine will."* (Dr. Gerald May) The only effective strategy for helping people change is one that empowers them to use the resources of the Gospel. Then change is not something to be feared but embraced.

If you're done changing....then you're DONE!

CHAPTER TWELVE

WARFARE OVER CHURCH ATTENDANCE

The closer we get to the coming of the end of this age, the more and more we see an apathetic attitude for and decrease in attendance in God's house. I have conversations with pastors all over the world. The one thing they all seem to complain about is how despondent and disinterested people seem in the things of God and His house. Yes, I am going to drive this nail. Yes, I'm going to bring it up. I've witnessed a terrible decline in the interest of the house of God in the last 20 years. People are too busy in their own little kingdom of their lives that they have completely forgotten God's house; yes, I mean church attendance. This is one of the greatest warfares we have to win.

It used to be that everybody had respect for church and church events and functions. I remember a day in this country when it was unlawful to be open on Sunday. It was called the Blue Law. Schools and businesses alike were sensitive to the meeting of the House of God in times past. As our society has moved further and further away from the things of God, we have moved further away from God's House.

I'm telling you right now we are in a battle over the gathering of God's people. The Kingdom culture is thinning out faster than we can build it. People are becoming more and more absent from the assembly. They are becoming more focused on their properties and needs and less on God's Word and House.

Yes, you can miss church at times and be okay. But I would counsel you to examine yourself closely. Ask yourself some pertinent questions. Do I make God's house a priority? Is my attendance growing weaker or stronger?

"Therefore, brethren, having boldness to enter the Holiest by the blood of Jesus, by a new and living way which He consecrated for us, through the veil, that is, His flesh, and having a High Priest over the house of God, let us draw near with a true heart in full assurance of faith, having our hearts sprinkled from an evil conscience and our bodies washed with pure water. Let us hold

*fast the confession of our hope without wavering, for He who promised is faithful. And let us consider one another in order to stir up love and good works, **not forsaking the assembling of ourselves together, as is the manner of some**, but exhorting one another, and so much the more as you see the Day approaching."*
Hebrews 10:19 -25

The Apostle Paul was warning us not to forsake the assembling of ourselves together. Then he makes a reference to some. He says, *"As some of you have been doing..."* (Paraphrasing)

Now don't you think that if Paul took the time to bring up this little rebuke that the gathering is important?

Where you place God's house on your priority list could be where God places you on His.

I was praying one day, asking God what is the real secret to prosperity. Why is there so much lack? Why do people work so much but have nothing to really show for it? I believe that the Lord revealed to me one of the greatest secrets to prosperity when He led me to read the book of Haggai.

*"A Message from GOD-of-the-Angel-Armies: "The people procrastinate. They say this isn't the right time to rebuild my Temple, the Temple of GOD." Shortly after that, GOD said more and Haggai spoke it: "How is it that it's the 'right time' for you to live in your fine new homes while the Home, GOD's Temple, is in ruins?" And then a little later, GOD-of-the-Angel-Armies spoke out again: **"Take a good, hard look at your life. Think it over!"***
Haggai 1:2-6 MSG

Here is where we need to stop for a moment. This is the Message Bible. The King James Version uses the phrase, *"Consider your ways..."* God says this statement two times. I believe that if God felt the need to say it twice we should stop and observe what He is really instructing us to do.

Consider your ways...focus and think about them. Stop what you're doing before it's too late.

Consider:

1. The course of life, mode of living, the actions and path you've chosen to walk.
2. Your conversations and what you keep saying about God in private. Pushing aside the need to be in His house for the needs of your own life.
3. Your customs and traditions. Don't allow the traditions of men to outweigh the Word of God. Customs can be hindrances if we don't keep the Word of God as our source.

In truth, we should break all customs and traditions when we enter into the blood covenant with Jesus Christ. We now forsake our own traditions and customs and pick up Kingdom customs and traditions.

Consequence for Ignoring God's House:

- You have spent a lot of money, but you haven't much to show for it.
- You keep filling your plates, but you never get filled up.
- You keep drinking, but you're always thirsty.
- You put on layer after layer of clothes, but you can't get warm.
- And the people who work for you, what are they getting out of it? Not much- a leaky rusted-out bucket, that's what.
- You have had great ambitions for yourselves, but nothing has come of it.
- The little you have brought to God's temple He has blown away—there was nothing to it.

*"And why? Because while you have run around, caught up with taking care of your own houses, my **Home (God's House) is in ruins**. That's why! I blew it away, **because of your stinginess**. And*

so I've given you..." Haggai 1:6-10 MSG

(NOTE: this is not the devils doing. This is not an enemy that you could so easily rebuke. This is the Lord's doing. No one can rebuke the Lord.)

- A dry summer and a skimpy crop.
- ***I've matched your tight-fisted stinginess*** by decreeing a season of drought, drying up fields and hills, withering gardens and orchards, stunting vegetables and fruit.
- Nothing—not man or woman, not animal or crop—is going to thrive. Haggai 1:11 MSG

I hope you saw it. God said He matched us in what we were doing. Matched has many meanings. It means to harmonize, to correspond with, and to do what you're doing.

God's command for prosperity:

" Then GOD said: "Here's what I want you to do: Climb into the hills and cut some timber. Bring it down and rebuild the Temple. Do it just for me. Honor me." Haggai 1:8 MSG

I like the NKJV; it says it this way...

" Go up to the mountains and bring wood and build the temple, that I may take pleasure in it and be glorified," says the Lord.

What is the purpose for the assembling? What is the real purpose for the house of God we call church? So that God can take pleasure in us and be glorified.

One of the greatest joys for a parent is to have all their kids and grandkids in one place. There's nothing like it; especially when they are in unity and in one accord. Sitting back and watching my children interact, laugh and fellowship brings such great joy to my heart. I can only imagine what God feels when He gets to meet with us all together. Yes, I love my children. Yes, I would go and see them individually; but there is something about all of us being together. There's chemistry, an air, an atmosphere that is greater than one at a time. The same is true for God's house; the church. When we are in one place together we get to increase the density of God in the atmosphere. Each one of us brings a piece of the Father with us. Together, He becomes weighted and dense. The power is in agreement.

There are two types of God's presence; His "**Resident Presence**" and His Omnipresence. I noticed that in the Garden of Eden wherever God was, that's where He communicated. Now, God is everywhere so when God told Adam to leave His presence He was referring to His concentrated presence. Adam had to leave where God had walked in agreement with him.

God speaks where His presence is concentrated.

His Resident Presence is the place where God inhabits. He is now abiding in one place. His presence is being pressed together to a density that the atmosphere is being filled with only Him. This is where the power lives. This residence is the church. The church is the Garden of Eden, where God wants to walk among His children again and speak. When God speaks, miracles happen!

Resident means a place where someone lives. It means occupant, neighborhood, local and present. God is increased as we gather. As we assemble, something happens. Didn't He say, *"Where two or three of you are gathered in my name, there I will be in the midst of you"* (Matthew 18:20)? Why can't we see this? Why are we arguing about this? What's the problem?

One day in prayer, God impressed on me the issue with the present day church. Remember this was what God spoke for me. I hope it will minister to you. Pray and let God speak to you.

Son, I see a great crisis in my house today. There is lack and weakness in some areas that need to be addressed...

1. There's **no conviction** anymore. Where there is no conviction there is no conversion. The sermons are becoming weaker and weaker. Grace has become an excuse to live poorly instead of being the empowerment I meant it

to be. I gave you grace, not so you would not sin, but to give you time to get your sin life dealt with.

I know this seems hard but look around. Monitor the way people live and act but still say they're okay. The church has gotten larger, but she has gotten weaker also. Never before in church history have we had such large and mega churches as we do today. More people are attending Sunday services, but we are experiencing few miracles. We are seeing no power. No one's being delivered. People are coming to an altar, getting baptized, but no one is changing. There's no conviction. People don't feel bad for doing bad things anymore. We must awaken mans' conscience. Conviction was God's way of changing people.

2. There's **no reverence** for God. The people are becoming like those in the wilderness who decided to build their own religion and made for themselves a golden calf to worship. What they wanted was a God they could see, a God they could control, a God they weren't afraid of; but the beginning of wisdom is to fear the Lord. (Proverbs 9:10, 1:7, Psalms 111:10)

Reverence means respect, admiration, worship, amazement and devotion. God is the God of all Gods, we should be honored that He's allowed us to meet with Him and to worship Him. It is very dangerous to attempt to make God your equal. I assure you, He is not!

3. People are abusing one another. When we abuse each other we are in reality abusing God.

4. No one wants to be like Me anymore. I am not popular to them. They want My acts, but they flee from My face. They want my favor, but not My fervor.

5. Everybody is in a hurry. So few want to wait on God. They want to come to His house and eat of His blessings but never wait for Him to enter the courtyard. We want the supply of goodness without the God who supplies them.

6. They can live in **fornication** and still act like they're okay with me. They're not. I have always given the instruction to restrain until covenant is made. Lying with someone before

covenant causes deep spiritual wounds. It takes years to overcome. Go back to the heart of My word. Refrain from such sins.

7. My people have become lazy and sluggish, while church buildings have become large. My church has mimicked the natural body. Obesity is killing the nation. Feeding the body without exercising its muscles causes people to become larger, but have less movement. It has happened to my temple as well.

Prosperity can be directly associated with our attendance to God's house. It is very important that you learn this principle early and not late. My Father use to tell me that church attendance is a habit. Get in the habit of putting God's house first. Make this a major priority. I promise you're going to see a drastic change in your increase.

CHAPTER THIRTEEN

WARFARE

OVER

YOUR HARVEST!

I often sit in amazement over how so many people in our churches become so aggressively angry at the teaching, preaching and mentioning of the prosperity subject. I have come to realize that they are not mad at increase or having more. Most of the hostility enters the conversation when I say you can sow your seed and expect God to return it to you in a harvest. Let me be specific! God will give it back to you with increase! People's countenance will change from joy to anger as soon as this one statement is mentioned. Some don't become angry, but they become confused and guarded.

It has been my experience that the warfare over a harvest isn't about people having, getting or needing more. People are okay with more as long as it is attached to their work, their efforts, their intellect, their bosses or even another person. The enemies' face surfaces when I tell people that God is the source of their increase!

Satan does not want us to become aware of the "**Seed Time Harvest**" principle. The reason why is because it places all the power of increase on your willingness to sow and all of your expectation on God to return it back to you multiplied. The Kingdom needs the message of harvest just like it needs the message of salvation. The King, Jesus, wants us to live and experience a life of abundance. We can do so much more to advance the Gospel when believers have more; *more money, more time and more resources*.

Think about this without fighting me! What could you do if you had more?

I was eating in a local restaurant one day with my wife, a friend and our grandbaby. I noticed a single woman sitting across the room eating all alone. Now, I hate to see people eating alone; it makes my heart heavy. So I kept glancing over at her, and thought to myself, *"Why don't you just buy her meal? Why sit there and just feel bad. God has blessed you... Release it!"*

I added this lady's meal and tip to mine when I went to pay. As I was leaving, I walked over to her and said, *"Ma'am, I want you to know I took care of your meal today."*

She looked up at me with tears in her eyes. Her replied got to me. She said, *"Sir, I was just sitting here praising God and telling Him how much I loved Him. He said to me, 'I know you do, and today your meal is on me.' Then you walked over here and told me you took care of me."*

Now, I was choked up! God trusted me to stand in for Him and to take care of someone He wanted to bless. I wasn't just willing to; I was able to release the blessing. I believe so many of us are willing to be God's hand of blessing. The problem is that we are not able to. Men's doctrines have outweighed the true *Word of God*. Give and you get it back with increase!

"Willingness means nothing, if you're not able."

I believe there are so many believers who are willing to be the hand of God to others. The reason they're not is because they don't have the resources to be one. They're willing but unable.

One night, I went to eat out with my family and friends. We took over the place! Now I don't like to wait, and I hate going to a restaurant and getting terrible service. Our poor waitress was working her fingers to the bone. I noticed she was the only person waiting tables. So I asked her, *"What's up with you being the only one waiting on all these tables?"*

She said, *"I'm so sorry for your wait. They have one cook, one hostess and one waitress."*

I watched her, and my heart felt heavy for her. She couldn't have been more than twenty four years old. I was filling out the credit card slip to pay and was going to put down a $20.00 tip for a $77.00 meal. I began to write the tip down and she said, *"Sir, you don't have to tip. Your dad already gave me $20.00 cash."*

I looked up at her and said, *"Well, I am going to tip you also."*

She said, *"Oh boy; I've not gotten a tip this big in so long."*

I looked at her and asked, "Is *that big to you?"*

She said, *"YES!"*

I crossed out the $20.00, wrote down $30.00, looked up and said, *"How about now*?"

She said, *"What?"*

Then I looked around and saw a guy I know sitting to my left. I asked him if he had paid his bill yet. He said, *"No, Bishop."*

I said, *"Don't; I'm paying for you and tipping for you, too."* His bill was roughly $13.00. So I paid it and added a $25.00 tip to his bill. Now the waitress's tip was up to $75.00 for that bill.

She looked at me and said, *"Why are you doing this*?"

I said, *"Because you matter to God. God sees you and loves you."*

With tears in her eyes she said, *"Can I give you a hug?"*

I said, *"I would love one!"*

Now, before we could exit the building, one of the people with my group told me that she had a three year old daughter. As soon as she told me that, the waitress had the little girl's picture out. She had the curliest red hair I've ever seen. My heart began to swell bigger. Christmas was just a few weeks away. I asked, *"Are you able to get your daughter everything she wants for Christmas?"*

She said, *"Well, she's only 3. I'm going to get her what I can afford and she won't know the difference."*

I said, *"I'm going to help you buy your child's Christmas."* That is exactly what I did. I want to meet the needs of others; not be in need. Could I have done that without the resources to do it? Absolutely not! *Willingness means nothing if you are not able.* I want you to win the warfare over your HARVEST! I want you to be able to meet the needs of others and not always live in need.

WARFARE AT MANY LEVELS

This is the truth and nothing but the truth. You're going to have to be able to withstand warfare at many levels to walk in a life that lives off the harvest. First, you're going to have to fight for your seed or over your seed. Secondly, you're going to have to fight the warfare over your patience. Thirdly, you're going to have to fight over your harvest. Harvest is one of the greatest things you can experience in life, but it is also the result of many days of sowing, watering, fertilizing, weeding and waiting. My good friend, Dr. Todd Coontz, said something to me years ago. It did not resonate in me at that time as it does today. He said, *"If you want to live a lavish lifestyle, develop sowing lavish seed."*

IF GOD IS LORD OF THE HARVEST, THEN WHO IS LORD OF THE SEED?

"...The harvest truly is great, but the laborers are few; therefore pray the Lord of the harvest to send out laborers into His harvest." Luke 10:2-3 NKJV

This verse gives us the distinction between what God is doing and what we need to be doing. God calls Himself Lord of the harvest; He is not calling Himself Lord of the seed. Jesus is King of kings and Lord of lords. He's the Lord of the harvest; we are the lords of the seed. The problem with the church is that we have attempted many things in the name of Jesus, but we fail to move into our authority and power to control our seeds. It is not that many of us are not sowing. We sow seeds every day. You are a walking warehouse of seed. You just don't know how to become strategic in sowing your seed.

You're sowing a seed every time you show kindness. When you do just about anything, most of the time that 'something' you are doing is a seed. Galatians 6:7 says, *"Do not be deceived, God is not mocked, for whatever a man sows, that he will also reap."* We have more power than we realize. Think about how powerful the seed is. We have been given the authority to oversee the seed's destiny. Jesus let us know what His responsibility is as the Lord of the harvest and what ours is by being lord of the seed. Jesus can't unlock what Heaven has for us until we unlock what we've been called to sow.

LEVELS OF WARFARE:

1. Warfare over your seed
2. Warfare over your patience
3. Warfare over your harvest

The reason there is so much warfare involved in this is because you will either live a life off your efforts or a life off your harvest. Harvest living is much better than having to live solely off your efforts. I believe the word that the enemy hates the most is SEED. God spoke to all three, who were present in the Garden of Eden, when He moved man from His garden to living outside of the garden.

"To the woman He said: "I will greatly multiply your pain in childbirth, In pain you will bring forth children; Yet your desire will be for your husband, And he will rule over you."" Genesis 3:16 NASB

"Then to Adam He said, "Because you have listened to the voice of your wife, and have eaten from the tree about which I commanded you, saying, 'You shall not eat from it'; Cursed is the ground because of you; In toil you will eat of it All the days of your life. "Both thorns and thistles it shall grow for you; And you will eat the plants of the field." Genesis 3:17-18 NASB

*"The LORD God said to the serpent, "Because you have done this, Cursed are you more than all cattle, And more than every beast of the field; On your belly you will go, And dust you will eat All the days of your life; And I will put **enmity** Between you and the woman, And between **your seed** and her **seed**; He **(the seed)** shall bruise you on the head, And you shall bruise him on the heel."* Genesis 3:14-15 NASB

Notice the word SEED! God exposed the way He was going to defeat the serpent on the earth was through *seedtime and harvest*. God uses this exchange in almost everything in the earth.

*"For as the rain cometh down, and the snow from heaven, and returneth not thither, but watereth the earth, and maketh it bring forth and bud, **that it may give seed to the sower,** and bread to the eater: So shall my word be that goeth forth out of my mouth: it shall not return unto me void, but it shall accomplish that which I please, and it shall prosper in the thing whereto I sent it."* Isaiah 55:10-11 KJV

I am aware that this passage is speaking more than just on seed, but it bears the burden to mention it. The whole earth's system is sowing to reap, doing to get, giving for more. The word is exchange. Of course, many have no problem with this philosophy as long as we keep it within the venue of man's efforts, man's energies and man's abilities. We receive no opposition as long as we keep the method of return in man's hand. Opposition arises as soon as we shift this seed teaching to sowing money seeds according to the law of the seed, into God's kingdom work and then place our expectations on God to return it to us according to Luke 6:38; *"Give, and it shall be given unto you; good measure, pressed down, and shaken together, and running over, shall men give into your bosom. For with the same measure that ye mete withal it shall be measured to you again."*

What's the one thing you really need to fulfill God's purpose and assignment on the earth? Yes, Jesus, the anointing and the calling are a given. But what else do you need? Resources... **MONEY!**

We are so afraid of talking about this. Money harvest is a great harvest. Without money all we can do is dream, wish and wonder. Yes, I want to address the warfare over seed, but I also want you to sow money seeds for money harvests. Stop trying to be super religious and say things like *"I'm not doing this for money or for anything but to please God."*

Deep down inside the place of our hearts, we don't want to talk about the fact that people are always saying and wishing for more money. If money wasn't a problem then there wouldn't be a problem giving it away.

MONEY WITH PURPOSE CREATES LASTING PROSPERITY:

It is having a purpose in life, not possessions, that are truly satisfying. Purpose can only be realized in the understanding and accepting of the person of Jesus Christ. Unbelievers often ignore the problems of prosperity and believers often ignore the purpose for prosperity.

MONEY MYTHS:
1. *Money is evil*. No, it is not. Money has no life, no will and no purpose. Money is an inanimate object. The only time money has a life is when it is placed in someone's hand. When it is put in the hand of the wicked then it pays for wicked things. When it is put in the hands of the righteous then it does righteous things.
2. *Money is of the Devil*. No, it is not! Although the system money travels in is a worldly system, it is not of the devil. If money was of the devil and the goal of hell is to destroy you, then why hasn't the devil overloaded your accounts with money yet? Because it is not of the devil. I'm not saying that money isn't dangerous. It is! Money can destroy you if you do not have good control of yourself and wants. That doesn't make it wrong; it makes you weak.
3. *Money can't make you happy*. Yes it can! Marriages end in divorce each year because of financial stress and lack. Money, in the right life, makes that life much happier. I have been on trips with little to no money and then I have been on trips where money was in surplus. I can testify right now that those trips with money in abundance were much happier and more fun than those trips where it was in limited supply.

~ 137 ~

I'll never forget one trip we took to Myrtle Beach with some friends of ours. My family of four was on a limited financial budget. The family we were hanging with was not. Everyone wanted to go to Ripley's Aquarium and that place isn't cheap. My wife and I decided to stretch ourselves and go, after seeing my childrens' faces and how excited they were. That was it...the money to get in tapped us; there was no money for anything else in the place.

My son loved this place. He became so interested in the sharks and the whales. The exit is located in the large gift shop, so we had to walk through all these toys and fish stuff. Our friend's daughter walked over to her dad with this huge stuffed whale; my son was standing right beside her with that whale's brother in his arms. The whale was bigger than him. My heart swelled; I wanted to buy him that whale so bad. I was willing but not able. It was expensive. I looked at him and tried to sell him on something else...something cheaper, smaller...something less. He was stuck on that one whale. He wouldn't change his focus.

Isn't that what lack really does to us? It forces us to settle for less when God wants us to have more!

My son walked off holding that whale. He was not going to let it go without a scene, for sure. My friend walked over to me, touched me on the shoulder and said, *"Here."* I looked down, and he was handing me money to buy that whale. He said to me, *"I don't want you to disappoint your son. Buy that whale."*

Tears swelled in my eyes. My heart was full of joy but at the same time anger. Thoughts ran through my mind, *"I've preached a blessing gospel; I've lived a good life. Why am I not walking in the overflow?"*

I made up my mind that day that I wasn't going to be in this situation the rest of my life. I began to study, pray and ask the Holy Spirt questions. I remember one night saying, *"God, there's got to be more. There's got to be better than this."* It was those questions and desires that led me to the revelation that if you can turn what you have into seed, it will increase to what you have expected it to be. If you are willing to let it GO!

4. ***Money isn't important.*** Yes it is! Money is the power part of our world. We bargain, trade and exchange our way through life with money! Shelter, food, medical care, education and even self-preservation involve money. Money is a basic method of communication between human beings. Money talks in war or peace, love or hate.

5. ***God doesn't want us to have money.*** Yes He does! This is absurd. Some would even add ...too much money... but the answer is the same. Yes He does.
    a. ***God is your source. (Matthew 7:11)***
    b. ***God gives us wealth. (Deuteronomy 8:18; 2 Chronicles 1:12)***
    c. ***Money is simply a tool.***

Money in the hands of Christians is a major threat to Satan.

Do me a favor, please! Activate the principle today of tithing and seed-faith sowing. Stop allowing the enemy to control your financial destiny. You have the power within you, right now, to start this life changing exchange. Do it now! Begin to build an expectation for your future by sowing, giving and trusting God for the return.

I believe the reason so many are walking in lack in their church is because they fail to differentiate the natural from the supernatural. When we sow seeds in the natural. We sow natural seeds into the soil and gather the harvest from that same field.

The Kingdom is much greater than that. We may sow in one soil but God can, and usually does, return it to us through many different soils. When someone sows in their church they can't expect their harvest to happen in that field. They need to see that God is going to return it to them outside of those walls. God will use men to return it to us according to Luke 6:38, *"...will men give back to your bosom."*

If you are afraid to let go of what is in your hand, you will never reap a harvest.

Fear strangles the faith you need to release the little so that it can become much bigger. Fear of loss becomes greater than the power of expectation for more. I asked my mentor one day, *"How come it seems so easy for you to sow?"*

He said, *"Son, when you get a picture of your harvest and you see that it is bigger than what is in your present life, the easiest thing you will ever do is let go of your seed."*

6 PRINCIPLES FOR 100 FOLD RETURN:

1. **Sow when times are tough**. The natural tendency, in troubled times, is to hold your hand closed tightly, attempting to save up and survive your crisis. When lack attacks, attack back with your seed. We must send a message to the enemy and to the world that God is our source. This is exactly what Isaac did (Genesis 26), and it is exactly what the widow did in 2 Kings 17.

2. **Fight the urge to eat your seed**. The widow in 2 Kings 17 was in a famine and all she had was enough for one day. The man of God asked her to sow what she had so she could have more. He said make mine first. This widow had two options, and so do you. She could ignore the instructions of the man of God, eat her seed and die during the famine or she could obey the man of God and release her cake. She had to make a choice, even though she was living in fear. She let her trust in God's word outweigh her fear in her present situation. What are you going to do? *If you eat your seed, you will fertilize someone else's harvest...or you can sow your seed and reap your own harvest.*

3. **Lay hold of God's Word no matter what!** God has given us His promises throughout the Bible about abundance. Sowing places Him at the front end of our lives.
4. **Guard your mind when sowing in times of famine.**
5. **Position and prepare for God's outpouring**
6. **Never give up. Never take no for an answer.** Victory belongs to those who will not take "NO" for an answer.

The "Do nots" Of Sowing in Times of Famine:

1. Do not doubt the Word of God.
2. Do not listen to the opinions of others.
3. Do not believe the lies of Satan.
4. Do not look at your present crisis. Stay focused on God.
5. Do not let down your guard. Guard your ears and your eyes.
6. Do not speak words of doubt or fear. Wrong words can dig up your seed.

WEAPONS HELL WILL USE TO DEFEAT US IN BATTLE

Satan's greatest rouse is **FEAR!** Fear is a mirage from Satan. Satan attacks us with difficult circumstances hoping that in the natural we will begin to feel the situation more than we can believe in the revelation. He's hoping that in our feelings we begin to build a wall of fear and doubt. That is why Paul told us in 2 Corinthians 5:7, *"we walk by faith, not by sight."* We build our belief system in our circumstances when we base everything on what we are seeing in the natural. We close up when this happens. We shut down. We isolate. We stop doing what we need to do to win. We stop sowing our seeds. We stop sending up our praise.

The only two things that God mentioned in the Word that He remembers is our...

1. Praise
2. Giving

SEEDS OF ATTENTION

It requires sacrifice to praise and give. We usually don't feel like sending up praise when we come to church after a long week of trials and tribulations. So when we do, *it's our seed of attention*. The harvest is God's presence. He said, "I inhabit the praises of my people." We are made in the image and likeness of the Godhead. We were not made to praise but to be praised. This is why we live for compliments and affirmation. So when we offer up praise to God, we are actually going against our nature and submitting to God's nature.

Giving has the same power. People are more comfortable with the word giving, but I like to say sowing seed. We were created to reap. God planted the Garden of Eden and put man in that garden to reap from it. So when we give (sow) we are once again going against our nature. We are killing self and giving God His rightful place.

F-E-A-R: FALSE EVIDENCE APPEARING REAL

We must not react to our circumstances. We must fight fear. We are not to be moved by what we feel or see. We do not look at false evidences appearing to be real. Instead, we stand on the promises of God's Word. So when our bodies are screaming that we are sick, we are to scream back that by His stripes we are HEALED! When our finances declare that we do not have enough, we are to decree and declare that we will sow in famine and that there is no more drought or dry season. We will no longer settle for less. We are blessed! We should make the proclamation that the joy of the Lord is our peace, strength, and wholeness when our minds are echoing that we are depressed, lonely or a failure. We should answer with the voice of our spirit that joy comes in the morning when our soul cries out that it's midnight and there is no more light. People of God, it's time to fight and win over this warfare. It's time to walk in our faith and not our fears.

FEAR AND FAITH CANNOT LIVE IN THE SAME ROOM.

You can't have **REASON AND FAITH** in the same mind. Fear and faith are opposites. The proof of faith is fear. Faith will always activate fear, but they are opposites.

- Fear is Satan's SEED.
- Faith is God's SEED.

Whatever seed you allow to be planted will be the seed that takes root and grows in your garden. Change your seed if you don't like what's been growing in your life. Faith seeds produce faith. Fear seeds produce fear. Faith will bring about God's provision for provision. However, fear will do the opposite. Fear will bring about Satan's provision for oppression, lack and eventually, poverty and death. One will destroy the other.

Here's a great scripture to help. Romans 4:20-21 says, *"He (did not waver) staggered not at the promise of God through unbelief; but was strong in faith, giving glory to God; and being fully persuaded that, what He (God) had promised, He was able also to perform."*

It's interesting to note here that staggered (waver) actually means that Abraham didn't slide between two mutually exclusive objects. Abraham didn't allow fear to push him off the mountain of his faith and slide down the side to failure and lack. Since God has given us His most precious promise, we should not be afraid to act. We should walk in

1. Peace to prepare the fields for our seeds.
2. Position to sow our seeds without fear.
3. Provision to sow in an accelerated season.
4. Perpetual privilege of always having from God more seed to sow for more harvests.
5. Promised harvest...it is our guarantee from sowing.

FEAR AND FAITH ARE HUNG ON TWO HINGES

According to Romans 10:9, *we are to believe in our heart and confess with our mouths.* These are the two hinges the door of faith or fear hangs on. We are to believe in our minds; then we are to put these thoughts to words. This is exactly what happened in I Kings 18:42 where Elijah's servant kept saying he saw no clouds. Elijah made his confession of faith by making him go back and look again. The servant came back and said, *"I see something, it may be a cloud about the size of a man's hand."* Elijah said, -and here is the hinge - ***"Get up, eat, and drink; for I hear the sound of the abundance of rain…"*** He first believed it or he wouldn't have kept sending the servant back. He confessed it when all they could see was a glimmer of something that resembled a cloud.

There was a time in my life, probably yours too, when I was hanging on nothing. I sowed my last dollar, said my last word and hung to my last glimmer of faith. In my famine, I kept claiming the prosperity, the healing and the victory. Everyone around me thought I was crazy and that I wasn't living in reality! They thought I had lost my mind and wouldn't accept it was over.

I just kept lifting my hands and praising God. I kept allowing tears of worship to flow down my cheeks, and I kept sowing my money seeds with a heart of expectation.

Everyone may think you are crazy, but this is what Elijah did. It is what the widow did, the woman with the issue of blood did, the woman at the well did, and the man at the pool of Bethesda did! They are the ones who got their harvest and so will we!

Another weapon of Satan's is GREED. The only way to conquer this weapon is to GIVE!

Please fight the warfare over your harvest. Sow your seeds with the expectation for your harvest. It is important that you do.

CHAPTER FOURTEEN

WARFARE IS
OUR
DESTINY

Everyone at one time or another is going to experience spiritual warfare. 2 Corinthians 10:5 gives us a clear insight into this reality.

"For though we walk in the flesh, we do not war after the flesh:(For the weapons of our warfare are not carnal, but mighty through God to the pulling down of strong holds;) Casting down imaginations, and every high thing that exalteth itself against the knowledge of God, and bringing into captivity every thought to the obedience of Christ; And having in a readiness to revenge all disobedience, when your obedience is fulfilled." **2 Corinthians 10: 3 – 6 KJV**

The greatest warfare we will engage in will not be an enemy approaching us, but the enemy that is within us all...our minds! The truth is that God is in total control of His plans. What God has no control over is you and your life. You control your life, not God, and especially not the devil. I'm not saying that the enemy isn't working overtime to get you to destroy your life, but in the end everything we face and go through is the result of our decisions. These decisions happen first in our thoughts and our desires.

The enemy will try and get your mind in a place that you can't get over your last mistake, your last bad decision, and your last rebellious act; getting you to become obsessed at what you've lost and what you could've had. The words I'm looking for to describe this are guilt and grief. No human alive was built to carry yesterday's regrets, failures and stupid. That's why we have to learn how to move into the realm of the supernatural.

The first word in this battle is **strongholds.** We are to pull them down, not with fleshly weapons but, with Godly supernatural weapons. God has put inside of all of us the power to win these battles. What is a stronghold?

"A stronghold is a mind-set, impregnated with hopelessness, which causes us to accept as unchangeable something that we know is contrary to the will of GOD."

In the Greek, the word "stronghold" is defined as something that is fortified through holding it. It is a place that the enemy has set up a fortified position by where he sends out all his attacks. Strongholds start in your mind from:

Strong = Power
Hold = Grip
Strong + Hold = Power Grip

The next word is **imagination**. Where are these battles taking place? They are happening in the valley of your perceptions. Imagination is where the power of increase exists. This warfare is happening in the place where resourcefulness lives and the area of your creativity happens.

SIGNS YOU ARE LIVING UNDER A DEMONIC STRONGHOLD

1. **Disunity begins to surface in every good relationship**. You are manifesting a sign that you might be under a demonic strongman when you start experiencing arguments and disagreements with those who are good for you. When you start to make decisions to change and all of a sudden you find yourself in disunity with those God has placed to help you. Stop and get help. The strongman is trying to bring you out from under the covering of those who can help you conquer him.

2. **Apathy becomes an everyday attitude**. Apathy is simply another word for laziness, boredom, lethargy and indifference. Those who are being controlled by a demonic strongman can't help but feel apathetic. Every time you start to grow and you decide to do better, this voice, this feeling comes over you. It's like a voice in your head

saying, "Why bother? I've lost so much; I won't ever get back what I've lost!"

3. **Overwhelming since of despair**. No matter how hard you try, you can't seem to shake depression. This is the most powerful part of the strongman's stronghold over you; to keep you so down and so full of despair you can't see tomorrow's blessings because all you can see in your present is yesterday's losses.

4. **Uncontrollable anger.** Anger is a clue. Those who are always angry have revealed that they know they are in the wrong, they just don't know how to get out of it. This is why your weapons to fight are not fleshly. They are supernatural. You must use and work the power of the blood of Jesus.

5. **An uncontrollable urge to hang with the wrong people.** Satan wants you to be in the crowd of the cowardly; those who can't and won't live right. They become the voices that stir you and control you. No one can ever achieve and succeed in the company of the ungodly. Take notice how the wrong people show up every time you start to make right movement to the light. Old friends just come out of nowhere. You can be making great head way in your new decision to follow Christ when out of nowhere you run into an old acquaintance or friend. This is someone that you use to do what you shouldn't do with. Before it's over, you end up hanging out with them and all at once your attitude and heart begin to sour again. The strongman has once again used the stronghold in your imagination to defeat you. But praise God for His mercies. You're going to beat the **strongman.** *When God wants to bless you, He will assign right people to your life. When Satan wants to destroy you, he will assign wrong people to enter your life.* You must decide whom you're going to hang with. Better to be alone that to die in a crowd of the ungodly.

6. **An overwhelming feeling to run from all responsibilities.** When this happens you will find yourself becoming more and more attracted to drugs or booze. The

enemy wants you to numb your mind long enough so that he can dig a hole you may never get out of.

7. **You have this sense of wanting to fight accountability.**

Your weapons:

1. **The Word of God**. God's Word has this power to do certain things for you. The Word of God will edify your spirit. It will encourage your mind. It will exalt your soul and mind. The word of God will equip you for your next battle and evangelize you for change.
2. **The Church**. Yes, the church is a weapon. It will surround you with like-minded believers who will help you and not judge you to change.
3. **Worship**. One of God's most powerful weapons is worship. The strongman can't live in the atmosphere of worship.
4. **The Blood of Jesus.** The most important weapon! The Blood of Jesus wasn't shed just to get you out of sin. It was shed to give you power over the strongman.
5. **Prayer.** Prayer isn't telling God what you've lost. Prayer isn't someone laying on their faces for hours crying about their pains. Prayer is much more than that. Prayer is a weapon. Those who have learned how to use prayer have discovered that there are 7 strategic levels or prayer:

1. Strategic Warfare prayer is **<u>Authoritative</u>**. Paul said he was confident that when he prayed God heard him. *"And this is the confidence that we have in him, that, if we ask any thing according to his will, he hears us."* **1 John 5:14 KJV**

   "See, I have this day set thee over the nations and over the kingdoms, to root out, and to pull down, and to destroy, and to throw down, to build, and to plant." **Jeremiah 1:10**

"Behold, I give unto you power to tread on serpents and scorpions, and over all the power of the enemy: and nothing shall by any means hurt you." **Luke 10:19**

The Greek words that describe the word "authority" are freedom, mastery, jurisdiction, delegation and influence. Pray with **authority**!

2. Strategic Warfare prayer is **Combative**. We are in a war. We have to understand that every day we must be prepared for battle. The enemy isn't going to stop until He is thrown into the bottomless pit. The phrase **"Lord of Host"** appears 273 times in the Bible. Host means army. He is the Lord of the armies of Heaven. The Lord is a warrior. Read Revelation chapter 19...

"I saw heaven standing open and there before me was a white horse, whose rider is called Faithful and True. With justice he judges and wages war. His eyes are like blazing fire, and on his head are many crowns. He has a name written on him that no one knows but he himself. He is dressed in a robe dipped in blood, and his name is the Word of God. The armies of heaven were following him, riding on white horses and dressed in fine linen, white and clean. Coming out of his mouth is a sharp sword with which to strike down the nations. "He will rule them with an iron scepter." He treads the winepress of the fury of the wrath of God Almighty. On his robe and on his thigh he has this name written:

KING OF KINGS AND LORD OF LORDS.

"And I saw an angel standing in the sun, who cried in a loud voice to all the birds flying in midair, "Come, gather together for the great supper of God, so that you may eat the flesh of kings, generals, and the mighty, of horses and

their riders, and the flesh of all people, free and slave, great and small." **Revelation 19:11-18**

3. Strategic Warfare Prayer is **Intensive: We have to pray with intensity. Intensity is praying with passion. It is praying from your heart and not from some written prayer that someone else prayed years ago. The Bible calls it fervent prayer. The effectual fervent prayer of a righteous man avails much (James 5:15).** Intensive prayer is prayer that has passion and focus attached to it. When intensity is applied to prayer it becomes a prayer that is so convinced that our fervency in prayer makes a difference that not to pray with passion would assure us of the total absence of the results. Intensive prayer pleases God. When Jesus prayed in the garden He prayed with such intensity that his brow began to drip with sweat and blood. Jesus crying out to God with such fervency indicates that the warrior has finally reached the point of true desperation. Here's where we reveal our true determination. Here is where our resolve has been proven. God, we are at the end, but we are not going to quit.

4. Strategic Warfare prayer is **Confrontational:** Faith is really confrontational. When we pray with total faith we are actually praying a prayer that confronts the situation. In Acts chapter three, Peter confronted the crippled man. Peter used his faith. In Mark 11:23, Jesus admonishes His disciples to command mountains to move if they get in their way. Jesus' used this phrase to instruct them, "This Mountain." He was letting them know when you are speaking warfare prayer be specific. Identify the issue, the mountain and the crisis. Be direct in your authority to take these spiritual matters face on. Jesus tells us in John 14:3 *"... ask in my name... I WILL DO IT..."* In the Greek, ask isn't focusing on the question but rather on the authority of what you're claiming or demanding to happen

in Jesus' name. So when it happens, and I believe it will, you have only one person to praise. That person is JESUS.

5. Strategic Warfare prayer is **Comprehensive:** Extensive! Matthew 21:22 says, *"... and whatever things you pray..."* the word whatever is certainly comprehensive. We can have whatever we ask.

6. Strategic Warfare prayer is **Creative:** Creative prayer is prayer that allows us to become a part of God's creative process in bringing His purpose to pass. For creative prayer to work we must have that kind of creative faith. We are able to see the gain rather than the loss or cost of what we believe for. Romans 4:17 NKJV says, *"... in the presence of Him whom he believed – God, who gives life to the dead and calls those things which do not exist as though they did;"* Faith perceives that the thing we believe God for is real, and a fact that is not revealed to the human senses. Creative prayer sees into the impossible and calls the possible out of it. It is seeing into nothing and calling something into existence. How do we do this? We do this with our mouths; we talk, speak and pray the Word of God.

7. Strategic Warfare prayer is **Decisive:** When we are decisive in our prayers we dethrone the enemy and enthrone Christ in our situation. (I John 5:4-5; Romans 16:20; I Corinthians 15:57; II Corinthians2:14; Leviticus 26:7-8; Deuteronomy 20:1,4) Decisive means to be convincing.

Steps to Unlocking the Kingdom:
1. You must understand that what you see is not all you can have.
2. You must know who God is (Matthew 16:15). Jesus asked His disciples *"Who do you say I am?"*
3. You must believe that God wants to reward you and increase you.

4. You must be someone who is not perfect but who is diligently seeking God.
5. You must be an overcomer! (Revelation 1:18,19)

CONCLUSION:

I really enjoyed writing this book. My whole life has been a life of warfare and struggle. From as far back as I can remember I had to fight for anything I wanted. Let me encourage you. I am not a born warrior. I was the kind of kid who wouldn't fight. I ran from so many fights growing up. I was afraid of my enemies.

But now as an adult, I realize that it is far worse to run from a battle than to be beat up in one. Standing up for yourself or for what you believe in is far more gratifying than living a life always running from your crisis or battles. I'm not a born fighter, but through the power of the blood of Jesus, I've become a trained and anointed warrior.

If I can leave anything with you in this book, don't run from what needs to be confronted. You cannot win in life without warfare. Make up your mind that you're done running from the situations, crises and failures of life. You're ready - with God's help - to Stand, Fight and Win!

When you feel like no one is on your side, don't worry! God said He would never leave us nor forsake us. God will be your ever-present help in the time of struggle. He's faithful to us and to His cause.
Hang in there...God is sending help! Your victory is just around the next corner. Your season is changing today.

Dr. G

Sources

- http://www.divorcepad.com/rate/
- http://ezinearticles.com/?Single-Parent-Family-Statistics---Single-Parents-a-New-Trend?&id=1552445
- http://en.wikipedia.org/wiki/Battle
- **"The Believer's Identity in Christ,"** http://www.sw-mins.org/identity.html

- **"Knowing God."** http://www.sw-mins.org/strat4.html

MAY I INVITE YOU TO MAKE JESUS CHRIST LORD OF YOUR LIFE?

The Bible says, "That if you will confess with your mouth the Lord Jesus, and will believe in your heart that God raised Him from the dead, you will be saved. For with the heart man believes unto righteousness; and with the mouth confession is made for salvation." Romans 10:9, 10

PRAY THIS PRAYER WITH ME TODAY:

"Dear Jesus, I believe that You died for me, and that You rose again on the third day. I confess to You that I am a sinner. I need Your love and forgiveness. Come into my life, forgive my sins, and give me eternal life. I confess You now as my Lord and Savior. Thank You for my salvation! I walk in Your peace and joy from this day forward. Amen!"

Signed_____Date _____

☐   Yes, I would like to be put on your mailing list.

Name_____

Address_____

City_____State _____ Zip _____Phone:_____

Email:_____

FOGZONE MINISTRIES
P.O. Box 3707, Hickory N.C. 28603
1.888.328.6763 Fax: 828.325.4877
WWW.FOGZONE.NET

WHAT OTHERS ARE SAYING

Dr. Jerry Grillo lives what he teaches. It has been my privilege to be his personal friend for a number of years. He is a living example of a victorious leader. His church is a victorious church. If you can't succeed under this man of God you can't succeed anywhere. His revelation is life's fresh air in a stagnant world. He is one of the happiest and most exciting leaders I have known through my thirty-eight years of world evangelism. It is my privilege to recommend any book he has written.

> Dr. Mike Murdock
> The Wisdom Center
> Dallas, TX

Dr. Jerry Grillo is truly a gift from God to my life. I love his passion, his purity and his painstaking commitment to purpose. It is very obvious that he loves the God he preaches to us about. Should you ever have the privilege of speaking into this life, you would know without a doubt he's one of God's favorites. Bishop Grillo, what a wonderful refreshing, what a wonderful friend!

> Pastor Sheryl Brady
> Sheryl Brady Ministries

Bishop Grillo is fast becoming a leading voice of authority... Having him minister at our Emotional Healing Conference became a valuable training session to our leadership and a needed breakthrough to many of our members. To say that Bishop Grillo is qualified to pen these pages would be an understatement. You hold in your hand a key to unlocking the life that God desires for you. I dare you to turn these pages with even the least little bit of expectation and watch as God begins to show out in your life!

> Bishop Jeff Poole
> New Hope International
> Warner Robins, GA

TO INVITE DR. JERRY GRILLO TO SPEAK AT YOUR NEXT CHURCH CONFERENCE, BUSINESS MEETING OR TO SCHEDULE TELEVISION OR RADIO INTERVIEWS

WRITE TO:

FOGZONE MINISTRIES
P.O. BOX 3707
HICKORY, NC. 28603

OR EMAIL: FZM@FOGZONE.NET

FAX INVITATION TO 828-325-4877

OR CALL 1-888 FAVOR ME

Dr.
Author, Pastor, and Motivational Speaker

Favor Conferences - Dr. Grillo is able to minister to many during seminars and conferences throughout America and around the world. Dr. Grillo's heart is to help encourage and strengthen Senior Pastors and leaders.

Books - Dr. Grillo has written over twenty-five books including best sellers, "Saved But Damaged," and, "Pray for Rain." Dr. Grillo sows his book, "Daddy God," into Prison Ministries across the country, this book shows the love of God as our Father.

Internet and Television - Dr. Grillo is anointed to impart the wisdom of God on Favor, Overflow and Emotional Healing. Online streaming and television has made it possible for Dr. Grillo to carry this message around the world into homes and lives that he would otherwise not be able to reach.

Dr. Jerry Grillo
STREAMING
Miss your local church service?
Watch Dr. Grillo online, and
see him LIVE
Sundays @ 10:30am EST &
Wednesday @ 7:00pm EST

@BISHOPGRILLO

/BISHOPGRILLO

GODSTRONGTV

Join the
FAVORNATION
by texting
FAVORNATION
to "22828"

STAY**CONNECTED,**
BE**BLESSED.**

From thoughtful articles to powerful newsletters,
videos and more, www.fogzone.net is full of
inspirations that will give you encouragement and
confidence in your daily life.

AVAILABLE ON WWW.FOGZONE.NET
to Join the FAVORNATION and receive a weekly update
text the word "FAVORNATION" to 22828

LAUNCH
PASTORS AND LEADERSHIPS

Weekly Conference Calls from
Dr. Grillo will help you grow
in your relationship with the Lord
and equip you to be everything
God intends you to be.
Wednesday @ 12:00pm EST
Call: (712) 432-0075   Playback: (712) 432-1085
access CODE 138750#   access CODE 138750#

Dr. Jerry Grillo
STREAMING

Miss your local church service?
Watch Dr. Grillo online, and
see him LIVE
Sundays @ 10:30am EST &
Wednesday @ 7:00pm EST

Dr. Jerry Grillo
VIDEO ARCHIVE

The Video Archive is a great
way to watch Dr. Grillo where
you want and when you want.
Go to www.drjerrygrillo.com
and click on "Encore"

CONNECT WITH US

Join the
FAVORNATION
on your
favorite social
network

PUT DR. GRILLO IN YOUR POCKET

Get the inspiration and
encouragement from Dr. Jerry
Grillo on your iPhone, iPad or
Android device! Our website will
stream on each platform.

Thanks for helping us make a difference in
the lives of millions around the world.

WWW.FOGZONE.NET